CONTROLOLOGY

Beyond the New Criminology

Jason Ditton

First published 1979 by
THE MACMILLAN PRESS LTD
London and Basingstoke
Associated companies in Delhi
Dublin Hong Kong Johannesburg Lagos
Melbourne New York Singapore Tokyo

Photoset by Vantage Co. Ltd,
Southampton and London

Printed in Great Britain by
Billing & Sons Limited, Guildford, London and Worcester

British Library Cataloguing in Publication Data

Ditton, Jason
Controlology.
  1. Deviant behavior   2. Social control
  I. Title
  301.6'2   HM291

  ISBN 0-333-25965-3
  ISBN 0-333-25966-1 Pbk

Contents

Acknowledgements   iv

1   THE CONTROLOLOGICAL PEDIGREE   1

2   CRIME WAVES OR CONTROL WAVES? A
    RECIPE FOR ATHEISTIC STATISTICIANS   8

3   'MR BIG' AND 'THE GODFATHER': SHOP-
    PERS, DEALERS AND SQUEALERS AS
    DRAMATIC CHARACTERS IN A FACTORY
    CONTROL WAVE   51

4   'RESPONSIBILITY' VS. RESPONSE ABILITY:
    THE CONTROLOLOGICAL PROGRAMME   100

    Bibliography   109

    Index   121

Acknowledgements

Several people have been kind enough to read and comment upon parts of this book in draft form. Special thanks are due to Richard Brown, Stan Cohen, Paul Rock, Bob Roshier, Donald Roy, Laurie Taylor and Leslie Wilkins for providing a number of helpful remarks and suggestions which I have included without specific acknowledgement. In many smaller, but no less significant ways, I am indebted to Robin Williams and several other members of the Durham University Sociology Department, and to my new colleagues in the Sociology Department at Glasgow.

I have also benefited from a different sort of assistance from John Winckler at Macmillan, from Pru Larsen for some exceptionally competent typing and organisation, and from Elizabeth Baker for speedy indexing.

Part of this book was prepared whilst in receipt of S.S.R.C. Grant No. HR 3603/1.

University of Glasgow   JASON DITTON
July 1978

1 The Controlological Pedigree

> A fundamental direction that labelling analysis must take is toward the construction of propositions, which will make it more of a theory and less of an exercise in theorising. At the present time, labelling analysis consists largely of theorising, developing ideas that are not crystallised into theories but serve only to generate more loosely related ideas. (Ericson, 1975, p. 141).

The labelling perspective is dead: long live labelling theory. However, this book is a plea for reformulation, not one for resuscitation or rejuvenation. Rather than celebrate or bewail the currently morbid state of affairs, I hope instead to analytically reground the labelling approach. I think this is possible as labelling is vilified not so much because of its analytic inabilities, but rather because it has become an *institutional* failure. Since institutional failings are easier to correct than analytic ones are to patch up, there is still a chance that the magnificently imaginative scope of the labelling perspective might be refashioned as an intellectually and institutionally competent theory.

There are two interrelated elements of this institutional failure. Firstly, the institutional failure *of* labelling. The labelling approach, with its concern with the broad category of social deviance, rejected rather than attempted to replace positivist criminology (with its narrow emphasis on crime). Accordingly, the neologism 'controlology' is stylistically and analytically designed to *replace* criminology. Secondly, there has been an institutional failure *in* labelling, which has remained a perspective, and never became properly organised as a theory. In this latter sense, controlology is the basis for an analytic programme evolved to convert that perspective into a theory.

One way of considering this sort of development is by co-opting Kuhn's (1970) attractive analysis of the development of what he calls 'mature sciences'.[1] Although the validity of applying that analysis to the social sciences has been (quite rightly) doubted,[2] it is at least roughly adequate as a sensitising descriptor of the development of criminology and of the sociology of deviance. Kuhn's analysis is schematised in Fig. 1.1, below, and a slightly modified version of it, when applied to criminology, is provided in Fig. 1.2, opposite. There is no space here for a detailed justification of this application nor, for that matter, for a substantial

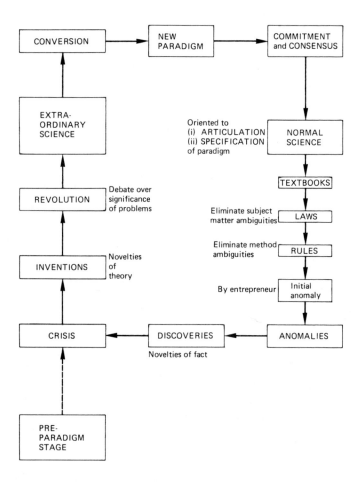

FIG. 1.1 *Kuhn's developmental pattern of future sciences*

account of the drawbacks of and difficulties with the labelling perspective. The first would be a lengthy task, and quite unnecessary given the rather slight purpose of its use here; and the second has been offered so frequently,[3] and occasionally adequately elsewhere,[4] as to make yet another version here simply confusing and redundant. Instead I shall just hang what are for my purposes the relevant parts of the history of criminology and of the sociology of deviance on Kuhn's analytic structure.

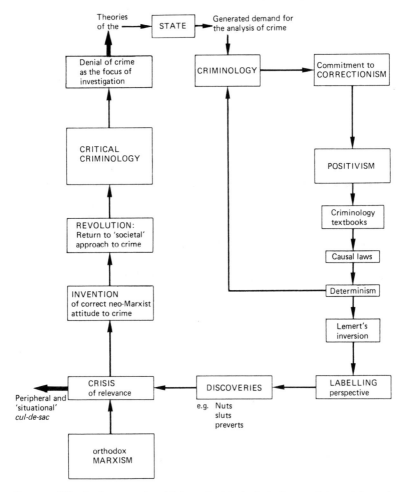

FIG. 1.2 *The development of positivist and critical criminology and the sociology of deviance*

Maturing suspicion of the continued competence, coherence and relevance of positivist criminology crystallised in the early part of the 1960s around Edwin Lemert's somewhat later anomalous inversion of the conventional relationship between deviance and control. He said (1967, p. v):

> Older sociology . . . tended to rest heavily upon the idea that deviance leads to social control. I have come to believe that the reverse idea, i.e., social control leads to deviance, is equally tenable and the potentially richer premise for studying deviance in modern society.

The enchanted triumvirate of Matza, Becker and Lemert might best be viewed retrospectively as having formed the labelling school loosely around this core theme. But apart from shaky attachment to the key anomaly, the followers of (what must have seemed to conventional criminologists as) this incredible eclectical conspiracy had little else in common. Behind the labelling flag assembled scholars from a multitude of disciplinary origins, embracing a multiplicity of epistemological orientations, suffering from an extraordinary lack of analytic agreement, and pursuing an enormous and catholic range of methods.[5]

However, subsequent repair of the new paradigm was lacking in the critical element necessary to shift the emergent discipline into what Kuhn refers to as 'normal science'. Granted, colossal substantive specification of the paradigm followed immediately with the discovery of the assorted rag-bag of what one critic has referred to as the 'nuts, sluts and preverts' (*sic*) of society;[6] and admittedly some of the substantive contributions contained snippets of analytic refinement which might be seen as specific peripheral articulation of the paradigm.[7] But general, *central theoretical* articulation has always been absent. Some 'textbooks' professing claims to offer such a contribution seem only to be stylistically elegant recasting replications of the original works,[8] collectively displaying widespread disagreement. Serially assembled sets of edited readings (rather than cumulatively informed textbooks) formed the institutional foundation of labelling, with each set of readings embracing a minutely varied slant, although often despatching the same tired articles to do their duty before a new batch of students.[9]

A new growth industry has been based upon critical refutation of elements of the labelling perspective[10] (to which some of the originators have variously replied);[11] and this has been more recently supplanted by attempts at creative replacement of labelling with the 'new' or 'critical' criminology.[12] The current situation is one of diffident squabbling between potential alternatives to conventional positivist criminology, with the 'alternatives' attracting most of the brains, and the conventional school (still, unfortunately) attracting most of the money and power. True to form, the Marxist critical alternative, like its labelling predecessor, has begun to attract a deadweight of critical critics.[13]

As Fig. 1.2 tries to display, conventional positivist criminology trundles laboriously, endlessly and (in terms of the picture of the subject matter it purveys) essentially mindlessly around the institutional circuit of power and repression. The total rejection of positivism by followers of the labelling perspective either had no effect at all on the institutionalised study of crime or, at best, the massive theoretical critique was distilled into an additional factor ('the reaction'), to be henceforth co-opted in the unchanged rhetoric of mathematical calculation. In those research centres established before the early 1960s, criminology has continued to mean correctionism, positivism and determinism. The labelling perspective, with its continued emphasis upon what Plummer (1978) refers to as 'situational' to the neglect of 'societal' aspects of deviance, has never contained a sound basis for a full-frontal displacement of institutionalised criminology. It has always been content instead to snipe at convention from the theoretical sidelines – happy to stand on the lunatic fringe and lob distracting stories of strippers, nudists, gays, teddy-boys, nutters, dwarfs and druggies at the central juggernaut of state-sponsored criminology – and never keen to enter the heavy theoretical fray. Two of the big three have left the arena (Becker to the sociology of art, Matza to labour history), leaving Lemert alone to carp episodically about the trendy triviality of the work done (partly) in his name. Persistent general failure to substantively engage central areas of popular concern (murder, violence and theft) by the labelling school, coupled with a failure to rise above purely phenomenal analysis, has forced traditional labelling out of the mainstream, and left it idling in an historical *cul-de-sac*. The immediate response to some of these failings – critical criminology – rediscovered the 'societal' approach, but became almost instantaneously footloose by rejecting a centralised concern with crime, and

neglecting to continue the battle with criminology, and by career-
ing instead off the circuit into a relatively orthodox analysis of the
state.

   In these terms, controlology is aimed at rectifying an institutional failure within labelling, through central theoretical articulation of Lemert's revolutionary and anomalous inversion of the
conventional crime/control equation. I shall produce this articulation through a societal, rather than situational 'theorised ethnography' of the control of two despatch workers who were sacked
for stealing from the Wellbread bakery when I was working there
in 1973.[14] Chapter 2 contains the theory: and Chapter 3 the
ethnography.

NOTES

1. For alternative histories; see Levin and Lindesmith (1937), Matza (1969),
   and Cohen (1974).
2. Robert Friedrichs's attempt (1970) to apply Kuhn's analysis to the study of
   sociology did not receive much sympathetic acclaim (see Masterman, 1970).
   Edwin Lemert nevertheless applied the model successfully to the history of
   the American juvenile court (Lemert, 1970) demonstrating that the model
   may successfully be applied to the history of the positivistically based
   institutions – as I hope to do here.
3. See the items listed in note 10 below.
4. Particularly by Geoff Pearson (1975) and Richard Ericson (1975).
5. For me, Becker (1963, 1967), Matza (1964, 1969) and Lemert (1951, 1967)
   are the key personnel, with Schur (1965, 1969) and (1971), Scheff (1966),
   Erikson (1962), Kitsuse (1962), Goffman (1963) and Sudnow (1964) in the
   second rank.
6. See Liazos (1972); for another, similar account see Hagan (1972).
7. Attempts at empirical confirmation would appear both pointless and common. See R. Ball (1966); Gibbons and Rooney (1966); Priest and McGrath
   (1970); Brennan (1974); Nettler (1974); Rodgers and Buffalo (1974); Rotenberg (1975). Pro-labelling works containing peripheral analytic refinements
   include: Trice and Roman (1969–70); Turner (1971); F. Davis (1961); Katz
   (1972–3, 1975); Newman (1973); Rotenberg (1974); Rodgers and Buffalo
   (1974a); and Levitin (1975).
8. For example, Lofland (1969); Box (1971); Rock (1973a); Taylor (1971); and
   Quinney (1970).
9. For example: Becker (ed.) (1964); Wolfgang, Savitz and Johnston (eds.)
   (1962, 1962a); Rubington and Weinberg (eds.) (1968); Cohen (ed.) (1971);
   Filstead (ed.) (1972); Douglas (ed.) (1970, 1970a); Taylor and Taylor (eds.)
   (1973); Rock and McIntosh (eds.) (1974); Radzinowicz and Wolfgang
   (eds.) (1977, 3 vols).
10. For example: Gibbs (1966); Gouldner (1968); Akers (1967–8); Gove (1970);

Mankoff (1971); Gibbons and Jones (1971); Warren and Johnson (1972); N. Davis (1972); Hagan (1972); Liazos (1972); Rock (1973, 1974); Schervish (1973); Thio (1973); Goode (1975); Hirschi (1973); Broadhead (1974); Manning (1975); Pearson (1975); Beyleveld and Wiles (1975); Wheeler (1976); Fine (1977); Walker (1977); Knutsson (1977).

11. See: Becker (1970a, 1973); Lemert (1974); Schur (1971); Kitsuse (1972); Scheff (1974).

12. Although some work in this (essentially Marxist) tradition is *applicative* – e.g., Gordon (1971, 1973); Pearce (1976); and Chambliss (1964, 1971, 1975) – most is basically *stipulative* – e.g., Taylor, Walton and Young (1973) & (eds.) (1975); Sumner (1977); Spitzer (1975); Doleschal and Klapmuts (1973); Chambliss (1975a).

13. See, in particular: Hirst (1975); Rock (1973b, 1977); Atkinson (1974); Sykes (1974); Bankowski, Mungham and Young (1977); Steadman-Jones (1977); Coulter (1974); Mugford (1974).

14. See Ditton (1977), ch. 1, for an account of 'theorised ethnography', and of the Wellbread Bakery. For some more specific information about the research there, see note 1 in Chapter 3.

2 Crime Waves or Control Waves? A Recipe for Atheistic Statisticians

The crucial proposition of the labelling perspective was that rather than crime being unquestionably generative of control, (maybe) ironically, control produced crime. Whilst tremendously influential however, the proposition has never been vigorously explored as part of a general theoretical structure. This gap may partly be explained by the overwhelming emphasis within labelling upon substantive specification, but mostly by the submerged epistemological hiatus which lay between Lemert's conventional (i.e., causal) phraseology – 'leads to', 'hypothesis' – and the radical (i.e., interpretative) allegiances of those who followed Lemert into the brave new world of labelling.

One relatively conventional criminologist who fortuitously bridged this gap was Leslie T. Wilkins. His concept of 'deviancy amplification' (Wilkins, 1964, pp. 90–1) – the application of some of the cybernetic principles of mutual causality developed by Maruyama (1960 and 1963) to the crime-control relationship – formed a link between conventional criminology and the new labelling perspective; and will provide the lynch-pin here of an argument designed to centrally articulate Lemert's key anomaly. The concept of deviancy amplification not only provided a competent theoretical grasp of some intriguing empirical discrepancies (on why the behaviour, for example, of heroin addicts differed markedly from continent to continent),[1] but also allied itself clearly with the spirit of 'scepticism' (Cohen, 1971, p. 14) which was sweeping the positivist cobwebs from the study of deviance. On top of this, it was substantively fertile. Wilkins's model spawned some of the more significant pieces of empirical work to emerge from the study of deviance, particularly Thomas Scheff's

8

(1966) American study of mental illness, Jock Young's (1971) study of drugtakers in London's Notting Hill, and Stanley Cohen's (1973) analysis of the English Mods and Rockers.

Wilkins's model offers a promising opening for the construction of a *theory* of labelling precisely because it demonstrates the irony of control simultaneously with its feasibility.[2] What follows below is an attempt to extend Wilkins's model to the point at which control may be seen to be operating *independently* of crime (rather than within a mutually causal framework) on the basis that such liberation will constitute an adequate propositional basis for a fully-fledged labelling theory.

(i) DEVIANCY AMPLIFICATION: SOME DIFFICULTIES

Extensive use of the deviancy amplification model has shown it, regrettably, to be a little threadbare at crucial points. Naturally, these need patching if the concept is to form the basis of a larger theoretical structure. To begin with, Cohen (1973, p. 198, emphasis added) describes a now familiar criticism:

> Although it is not implausible to suggest that something like this sequence [deviancy amplification] may have operated, one problem immediately apparent in any attempt to generalise too rigidly from it, is that *no readily available explanation exists as to how and why the sequence ends.*

There have been other criticisms,[3] and some empirical limitations of application of the model have been outlined.[4] However, the problem of the termination of the amplification sequence has remained as the greatest barrier to its universal acceptance.

Typically, this difficulty has been faced in an *ad hoc* empirical way. Cohen (1973, p. 199) suggests that amplification died out through 'simply a lack of interest' (by the media), and adds (p. 200) that (for the participants) '[t]here was a straightforward generational change in which the original actors simply matured out'. Cohen *does* hint at a wave of 'counter-suggestibility produced by the absurdity of some of the initial beliefs and a tailing off of interest' (*ibid*), but does not state whether or not this is either necessary or inevitable. Young (1971, p. 116) is a little miffed by the criticism and rejects it.[5] Society merely has to reverse the nature of control, he adds, and 'de-escalation' will occur. It is not, as I shall show, as simple as this. Taylor (and Robertson, 1974,

p. 116, and 1973, p. 63), like Cohen, notice that *in practice* (of course) amplification does not continue indefinitely, and that generally, although amplification replaces earlier stable (or easy) peace with a period of intolerant and unstable (uneasy) peace, original stability is eventually reinstated. To account for this, Taylor (1971, p. 72) proposed what he calls a visibility/accessibility 'thermostat'. He notes that stability may return because:

> Particular deviants' actions may, by their universalism or their private nature, become so inaccessible to social control that the amount of public concern expressed about them by the authorities is reduced lest continued evidence of the failure of the police and others to control the activity produce public alarm or disapprobation.

This is a neat formulation, but ultimately itself suffers the criticism it was designed to eradicate. It contains no possibility that control might actually *work* (i.e., that deviants cease to be deviant), and merely proposes that, relative to deviance, control loses all efficacy, and the deviants do it in private. Presumably, and here's the rub, thus unhindered by control, practising deviants would multiply – indefinitely.

But Taylor at least indicates his awareness that Wilkins's model is theoretically, and not empirically, inadequate. It is not that the cases of the drugtakers, or the Mods and Rockers contradict the usual run of things by eventually declining in numbers but rather that they are an *example* of the 'usual run of things', and that, on the contrary, it is the usual formulation of the *model* which is at fault. I shall try to show, however, *not* that the oft-cited empirically exogenous factors (the police 'lost interest', the media 'gave up', or the participants 'grew up') are irrelevant but, on the contrary, how predictable and logically flawless such responses are, being based ultimately, as they are, upon the operation of some inevitable and endogenous factors which I shall describe after dealing with some preliminary difficulties.

First, what *was* Wilkins's model? Derived theoretically from Maruyama (1963), and empirically from Kitsuse and Dietrick (1959), Wilkins (1964, p. 90) suggests a single-loop regenerative feedback deviancy amplification model[6] (see Fig. 2.1, opposite).

There are some immediately apparent ambiguities in Wilkins's formulation. It is not clear, at three distinct points (marked as (i),

(ii) and (iii) in Fig. 2.1), exactly what is going on. In fact, at each point, it is possible that one (or more) of *five* different 'things' are

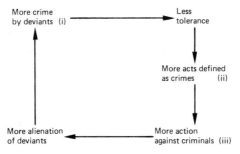

FIG.2.1 *Wilkins's simple amplification model*

occurring. In line with Wilkins's original 'regenerative' formulation, I shall refer initially to *in*creases in crimes, although (with the substitutions of the word 'less' for the word 'more', and 'fall' for 'rise' in the following list, as I shall later document), *de*creases in crimes are equally feasible. The five 'things' are:

(1) More originally defined non-deviant acts are *defined* as deviant (CONSTRUCTED Crime-rise).
(2) More of those acts originally committed are *discovered* (FANTASY Crime-rise).
(3) More (subsequently or originally) discovered deviant acts are officially *collated* (BOOK-KEEPING Crime-rise).
(4) More mass-media *coverage* of deviant acts (REPORTING Crime-rise).
(5) More originally defined deviant acts are *committed* (REAL Crime-rise).

Looking again at Wilkins's model (Fig. 2.1, above), 'more acts defined as crimes' (ii) could refer to a *Constructed, Fantasy* or *Book-Keeping*-rise (as long as we just limit 'defining' to official audiences); 'more action against criminals' (iii) could refer to a *Reporting, Constructed* or *Fantasy*-rise; and (i), 'more crime by deviants' would appear to refer to a *Real*-increase, but could actually refer to *any* of the possible rise sources, since it is always feasible that the statistics used to evidence a *real*-rise are contaminated. Acceptance of the latter qualifier casts doubt on our ability *ever* to 'know' that deviants are committing more crimes: in fact, it

is impossible to re-read existing data to evidence a *real* crime-rise
once any credence is attached to the other types of interpretation
(i.e., *constructed, fantasy, book-keeping* and *reporting* changes) which
can be attached to crime rate-movement.

It is at this conceptual point that the resolution of the difficulties I have noticed with Wilkins's amplification model coalesces
with the 'problem' of statistical evidence. The five 'things'
catalogued above amount to a systematic classification of the
sources of troubles experienced by users of official criminal statistics. Discussing these difficulties is hardly novel: realisation of
their existence was in fact almost concurrent with the publication
of the first criminal statistics,[7] and they have been consistently
used (with the statistics themselves) to cobble up competing
claims that the crime-rate is rising *or* falling – even when the
data-base is the *same* set of figures![8] Before opening an argument
that the only acceptable theoretical implication of this possibility
is to believe *not* that the received statistics are dirty or patchy data
in need of perpetual renovation or repair in order to approximate
more closely (albeit asymptotically) to a truth – the 'amount of
crime' – lying elsewhere: but instead, that they always correspond
exactly to that truth, let me example the 'things' which will
ultimately support that latter argument.

Constructed rises (more originally defined non-deviant acts are
defined as deviant) can stem from either legislative or judicial
moral enterprise. Legislative change appears more influential.
Both Chambliss (1964, p. 214) and Thompson (1975, p. 83, *et
passim*) note how the notorious 1571 vagrancy legislation, and the
1723 Black Act, contributed to a bulge in the criminal statistics;
Gillis (1975, p. 99) shows that an apparent crime-wave in Oxford
between 1870 and 1890 (32.8 offences per year in the 1870s to 72.7
offences per year in the 1890s) needs to be understood in the
context of an actual decline in indictable crimes and a massive rise
in the number of non-indictable juvenile categories like 'malicious
mischief' and 'dangerous play', and Du Cane (1893, p. 486) offers
a simple and conclusive demonstration of the effects of legislative
moral enterprise upon criminal statistics when he reports that
'offences against the Education Acts could not be committed
before 1870, but they count for 96,601 in [1890]'. Examples of
judicial moral enterprise are relatively hidden from history, but
probably contribute more to short-term fluctuations in the crime-
rate. One example is offered by Cohen (1973, pp. 101–10) who

has chronicled the punitive use of remand, the publication of the names of juvenile offenders, the issuance of warrants for the arrests of offenders' parents, and other judicial innovations implemented by local courts during the Mods and Rockers panic of the 1960s. Another example, this time of the repressive role of the judiciary in the mugging-wave experienced in England in the 1970s, is documented in Hall *et al.* (1978, pp. 30–3, 37–8).

Fantasy rises (more of those acts originally committed are discovered) occur when feelings of moral entrepreneurship infuse a greater degree of attentiveness in the deviant audience. The deviant audience appears in two guises: the citizenry, usually held to 'discover' 86% of events which eventually find their way into the criminal statistics (Bottomley and Coleman, 1976, p. 43); and the police, responsible for a smaller, 13% of 'discoveries' (*ibid*). Citizen-victims are commonly held only to officially report a fraction of those acts in which they might be defined to be a victim (Sparks, Genn and Dodd, 1977); Center and Smith (1973, fns. 78 and 79, p. 1063) note how citizen-witnesses may report more 'crimes' after successful police-community public relations campaigns; and Wallerstein and Wyle (1947, p. 109) have demonstrated the enormous scope possessed by citizen-offenders to report their offences should they be so motivated. The ability of the police to contribute to the crime-rate is, naturally, related both to their numbers, and to their enthusiasm. Inevitably, this is hardly a novel suggestion. As John Clay (1855, p. 75, emphasis added) put it some time ago:

> Two years before this time, however [i.e. 2 years before 1842] ... and owing, no doubt, to the growing (and providential) conviction of the necessity for such a measure, the county police force had been organised; and it was now found capable of arresting and of permanently subduing the dangerous spirits which had been excited into action. Under all these circumstances, therefore, a considerable increase in committals might be expected. *The zeal and activity of the new constabulary added to the number of apprehensions and committals, though there might be no corresponding increase of actual crime.*

Gatrell and Hadden (1972, pp. 352–5) have carefully documented the phenomenal rise in police numbers in the late nineteenth century (from 1000 policemen per 100,000 persons in

1860 to nearly 1400 policemen per 100,000 persons in 1890); Tobias (1967, pp. 296–308), in an excellent section appended to an otherwise offensive book, has shown how the rise in police numbers in Leeds between 1857 and 1875 affected the recorded crime-rate; and Gillis (1975, pp. 107–8) has linked a similar rise in police numbers to the apparent crime-wave that faced Oxford during the same period. Manning (1977, pp. 167–8) has described how engendered police zeal and enthusiasm may produce more arrests for one type of offence (with no additional patrolmen), and we may expect a staggering increase in prosecutions for obscenity and related offences in the Greater Manchester area for 1978 due to the moral crusading of Mr James Anderton, Methodist lay preacher and (more recently) Chief Constable (*The Guardian*, 31.12.77).[9] Sometimes increased police numbers coincide with a surge of enthusiasm, or with a rise in the civilian population at risk from police activity. For example, Malcolm Young (1977, pp. 56–8) notices that the increased arrest figures for the Northumbria drug squad – 7 in 1966, 220 in 1974 – reflects both an increase in the number of officers in the squad – from 2 to 18 in the 8 years – and an increase in the population scrutinised for offenders from just Newcastle to, in 1974, the whole of the rest of Northumberland, and major parts of Durham as well.

Book-keeping rises (more originally or subsequently discovered deviant acts are officially collated), stemming from differences in the way that criminal returns are requested or compiled, or alterations in the way that official statistics are collated, can emerge in several ways. Sometimes, a paper crime-wave can result from official categoric reordering or criminal statistics. Radzinowicz (1941a, p. 140) notices how the huge increase in the number of reported forgeries of notes and securities in Poland between 1932 and 1933 (from 1596 in 1931 to 5507 in 1933) chiefly reflected the decision taken in October 1932 by the Ministries of Finance and of the Interior to henceforth extend the definition of the forgery of notes to include those uttering forged notes. Subsequently (*ibid.*) a 'great number of cases of wilful and unintentional passing of notes was henceforth included under the heading of forgeries of notes and securities, and, in consequence, swelled the volume of forgeries of notes and securities reported'. Similarly Mannheim (1965, I, p. 114) notes that in the same year, 1932, the London Metropolitan Police decided to abolish the 'Suspected Stolen' book and henceforth recorded all theft reports as actual crimes. The dramatic rise in indictable crimes known (1931: 26,000 to 1932: 83,000) – a 320% increase – may be almost completely explained by this record-keeping change. As R. H. Beattie (1955, 1960) has shown, regional variations can produce phoney differences. Commenting on America, he says (1955, pp. 183–4):

> Since its beginning 'Uniform Crime Reports' has collected data on larcenies in two classes: that in which the value of property stolen was $50.00 or more, and that in which the value was under $50.00. This distinction is shown in the published tables covering individual police departments. However, when the summary information is presented all larcenies are lumped together and are included in the total figures which are nominated 'major' crimes. In the annual bulletin for 1953, it is stated that 'major' crimes reached a new high of 2,159,000 in 1953, and yet included in this figure were over 900,000 offenses of larceny of property valued at less than $50.00. The inclusion of these petty larcenies in the total of figures for major crimes in the United States seems quite inappropriate and misleading. [(fn. here) In California larceny of property values [*sic*] at less than $200 is with few exceptions defined as petty theft. Less than ten per cent of all larcenies reported by California police agencies are other than petty theft. If the California definition were applied to the United States as a whole, and only ten per cent of the larcenies reported were considered serious or major crime, the number of estimated major crimes in the United States for 1953 would be only 1,000,000 rather than the 2,159,000 cited in the 'Uniform Crime Reports'].

In the U.K. the significant rise in the numbers of new heroin addicts which took place in 1968 and 1969 – the numbers rose from 664 in 1967 to 1476 in 1968, and 1030 in 1969 – chiefly reflected the 1968 official regulations making the registration of addicts compulsory for the first time (C.O.I., 1973, p. 6; see also Scull, 1972). More recently Sparks, Genn and Dodd (1977, fn. 8, p. 161) have noticed:

> [a] change in police recording practice introduced at the beginning of 1972: Home Office instructions provide that thefts (other than motor vehicle thefts) of property worth less than £5

in value are no longer recorded as 'crimes known'. At a national level, this change resulted in a substantial amount of phoney decriminalisation, since there were no less than 328,257 such offences known to the police in England and Wales in 1972; including those offences in the published statistics for that year would have raised the number of 'crimes known' by about 24 per cent.

Apart from changes in the rules for the eventual collation of statistics, there is also mounting evidence of variation and selectivity in the initial compilation of criminal returns by police officers. Black (1970, p. 735) discovered that American patrolmen do not record as many as 36% of crimes reported to them, and Coleman and Bottomley (1976, p. 348) have recently estimated that in one English city 9% of citizen-crime reports are similarly dismissed. This sort of police *under*reporting is frequently exacerbated by police *mis*reporting – with Ferracuti, Hernandez and Wolfgang (1962, p. 116) demonstrating that 70% of one sample of policemen misclassified one or more offences reported to them. An alternative source of paper crime-waves (and a growing problem) lies in the proclivity of policemen to fraudulently manipulate the crime data at their disposal. Both Bell (1960a, pp. 152–3) and Douglas (1971, p. 88) notice this in passing,[10] and Seidman and Couzens (1974) and Center and Smith (1973) have recently published detailed analyses of crime-data falsification by policemen in league with politicians in America. A final, and tricky, source of paper crime-waves foreshadows the 'atheistic' approach to official statistics which I shall detail shortly. Walker (1971, pp. 24–5) asks:

> A referee is attacked by ten spectators. An advertiser causes a fraudulent advertisement to appear in sixteen issues of *The Times* and defrauds eighty people. A father has sexual intercourse with his daughter ten times before his crime comes to light. A postman steals letters which he should have delivered to twenty-seven householders. A cashier pockets small sums of money each week. A burglar breaks into a hotel and takes property from ten guests. How many crimes are involved in each case?

After the Perks Committee on criminal statistics, the Home

Office formulated detailed 'counting rules' (see Baldwin and Bottoms, 1976, p. 40) to tackle this problem. A recent newspaper report indicated that this has not been particularly successful,[11] an outcome which is hardly surprising, given that according to one perceptive observer (Stamp, quoted in Seidman and Couzens, 1974, p. 485):

> The Government are very keen on amassing statistics – they collect them, add them, raise them to the nth power, take the cube root and prepare wonderful diagrams. But what you must never forget is that every one of these figures comes in the first instance from the . . . [village watchman], who just puts down what he damn pleases.[12]

Reporting rises (more mass media coverage of deviant acts) are a source of persisting bias (see Glasgow University Media Group, 1976, I, p. 167; and Emerson, 1975, for detailed discussions of this) generative of popular myths and proprietor's profits. Bell (1960a, p. 151), for example, recalls:

> [a] competition between newspapermen [which] generated a 'crime wave' by taking run-of-the-mill burglaries off the police blotter and featuring them in black headlines. The 'crime wave' ended when Theodore Roosevelt, the police commissioner at the time, called off the competition.

Reporting rises do not directly affect the criminal statistics, but may indirectly sponsor legislative and judicial change, fuel and direct police enthusiasm, and bring about book-keeping alterations.[13] Of *Real* rises (more originally defined deviant acts committed) there can, alas, be *no* evidence. This is obviously an important point, and the next section will be devoted towards its justification.

(ii) THE MYTH OF THE 'DARK FIGURE' OF CRIME

It is an historic failing of proponents of the labelling perspective logically to establish the conceptual status of official statistics for that perspective. For the establishment of a labelling theory, a basic reconceptualisation of the nature of official statistics is essential. Although Kitsuse and Cicourel (1963) established an early programme for such a position, because so few have been prepared to wholly relinquish official statistics as resource (or treat them ethnomethodologically as a topic), the analytic status of official statistics remains abysmally deficient and wretchedly ambiguous. Kitsuse and Cicourel in fact utterly disestablished the sophisticated positivist position (which held, in principle, that the official statistics were merely empirically incomplete in some way), and implied that the operation of the 'things' I have already exampled totally disqualify official statistics as an analytic resource, rather than simply partially limiting their utility. Biderman and Reiss (1967, p. 2) have usefully classified the conventional positivist attitude to official statistics as the 'realist' position (which emphasises the offence), and the ethnomethodological critique of Kitsuse and Cicourel as the 'institutional' one (which concentrates upon the reaction). However, Coleman and Bottomley (1976, p. 34) have drawn attention thus to the subsequent 'unsatisfactory state of affairs':

> Somewhat paradoxically, however, many of the scholars and researchers within the new 'institutionalist' tradition do not seem willing or able to follow through their position to its logical (and sociological) conclusion, as expressed by Black; despite the claim to treat the crime rate as 'a social fact, an empirical phenomena with its own essential integrity', and as an aspect of social organisation which 'cannot, sociologically, be wrong', much of the writing in the field still concentrates heavily on aspects of 'bias', selectivity and discriminatory handling by law enforcement and penal agents, in a way not very far removed from the assumptions of the earlier 'realist' tradition, in which crime statistics were regarded as providing an inaccurate picture of the 'real crime rate'.

Even the more sophisticated, up-to-date and radical proponents of labelling adhere to a curiously archaic (and in principle *anti*-labelling) view of crime-rates. Box (1971, pp. 68–9) is a good example. He says:

> Crimes officially known to the police must be an *unknown and unknowable* proportion of the total number of crimes committed. That is, since the 'real' volume of crime remains *unmeasured*, and, given present research techniques and ethical limitations, *unmeasurable*, there is no possible method of estimating accurate-

ly the proportion that is officially recorded. On the best available evidence, it is clear that the official statistics are deficient to the extent that they do not provide us with anything like an accurate index of the volume of crime being committed.

This may have seemed like a critical position: it is in fact an establishment one – and more than that, a conventionally positivist one. It may have seemed expedient to accept that there exists a 'dark figure' of crime (crimes committed but not collated in official statistics),[14] but that acceptance implied an inevitably conventional epistemological conception of the problem. As Larner (1977, p. 8) has said:

> There is a positivistic assumption behind this concept of the 'dark figure' which needs examining. In so far as a dark figure indicates a certain number of prosecutions for which the record has been lost . . . it is an acceptable convention. In so far as it refers to the number of times that the crime or crimes in question have been committed this is quite another matter. It gives an objective status to the crime which it may not deserve.

However, like Box, other labelling theorists adopted a new version of the old 'realist' position (new only in the substantive sense that 'inadequacies' were class biased), perceiving the lack of fit between official and 'actual' rates of crime to be a methodological misfortune, and not, as Kitsuse and Cicourel (1963, p. 247) had urged, as 'a matter of differences concerning the definition of deviant behaviour'. Admittedly, preliminary exhortations to 'take care' when dealing with official statistics increased,[15] but no one bothered to consider the logical implications of this attitude to official statistics for the development of the labelling perspective.

To do so requires a *conceptual* analysis of the 'dark figure'. As Sellin (1951, p. 64) has noticed, 'more research is needed on these theoretical problems of criminal statistics, however', and as Leslie Wilkins has said elsewhere (1965, pp. 277, 278), 'the main problems concerning criminal statistics are not matters of detail but relate to quite fundamental concepts . . . it is doubtful whether it is legitimate to discuss the concept of crime as though it was something which can be measured or counted'. What are these 'fundamental concepts'? The crucial (and from an authentic labelling vantage point, erroneous) conceptual underpinning of the idea that a 'dark figure' of crime exists is that a criminal act can be said to have taken place even if nobody has 'reacted' to it. Self-report and victim studies are then used to count those crimes which have slipped the official enforcement net: the basis of that as a methodological device being that it is offenders who 'commit' offences. This is anathema to a logically complete labelling position. The positivist defence to the labelling attack of the 1960s was to treat the reaction as just another factor to be inserted into the calculations. This bastardisation of the meaning of labelling can only be overcome by the realisation that the reaction is *constitutive* of the criminal (or deviant) act. In fact, the reaction *is* the 'commission' of the act. Accordingly, the *idea* of a 'dark figure' of offences committed without a reaction is an unnecessary absurdity. As Atkinson (1978, p. 66) has recently put it, 'the "dark number" . . . is only a problem if the investigator starts from the assumption that some "real" or "true" rate is approximated by the official rate'. The 'dark figure' is an absurdity, moreover, not without intrinsically conservative political functions.[16]

The source of this piece of positivist mythology can be traced, I think, to Howard Becker's (1963, p. 20) original inclusion of 'secret deviance' in his sequential model (later perpetuated by him in the category of the 'potentially deviant', described in Becker 1973, p. 44). Given that actors may be 'falsely accused' of crime (another of Becker's original categories), there is no need – indeed, it is theoretically impossible – to specify a pre- or potentially deviant population. After Wittgenstein, we may say the category of acts which may be labelled criminal (or deviant) is the category: 'any' acts.

I am not trying to say that acts (like cannabis smoking) are not enacted. Nor am I trying to pretend that cannabis-smoking is always and inevitably 'caused' by control. One can even verify, in various ways (perhaps), that more people smoke more cannabis more often in 1978 than was the case in 1958. This, even if it could be demonstrated, regrettably tells us nothing about crime. No 'crime' has been committed (in law and in logic) until a court finds – i.e. *creates* for all intents and purposes – guilty intent.[17] Accordingly (sociological) 'evidence' adducing the spread of cannabis use is not the same as, nor may it be substituted for, a legally acceptable and accepted evidence that a crime has been committed. The former rests upon the behaviouristic counting of acts: the latter upon a legal finding of guilt. Crucially, for the latter to be found, a transaction must occur between those validated to find guilt (the judiciary) and those on whose behalf that guilt may be found (potential offenders).

What is critical to this argument is that the category 'potential offender' includes *all* society's members. Further, this remains the case whatever acts are enacted by individuals, since (to co-opt the paradoxical categories from Becker's sequential model) *any* act can be a crime (the 'false' accusation) and, equally, any act can [not] be a crime (the actor has – sociologically – 'got away with it'). So what, in *all* cases, makes an act a crime? *Control.* In sum, it is not the offend*er* who 'commits' the crime: it is the offend*ed.* The presence of the offend*er* is neither a necessary nor a sufficient condition for the finding that a crime has been committed. On the other hand, the presence of the offend*ed is* necessary (and may also be sufficient – as with coroners' courts) for a crime to be committed. The offend*ed* thus 'commits' the 'crime' – whilst possibly and incidentally, albeit in a different way, also committing the 'offender'.

With this in mind (along with the difficulties noted by Walker quoted on p. 16 above), to ask 'how big is the "dark figure"?' is to pose a question of the same logical order as 'how long is a piece of string?' or 'how many grains of wheat are there in a heap?' To this sort of question Winch (1958, pp. 71–2) has replied:

> The issue is not an empirical one at all: it is *conceptual.* It is not a question of what empirical research may show to be the case, but of what philosophical analysis reveals about *what it makes sense to say.* . . . . By how many degrees does one need to reduce the temperature of a bucket of water for it to freeze? The answer to that has to be settled experimentally. How many grains of wheat does one have to add together before one has a heap? This cannot be settled by experiment.

The 'dark figure' is thus in principle infinite. How many crimes are there? As many as you want (to react to). I will shortly define this as an *atheistic* position: such a stance involves acceptance of the proposition that the only 'real' crime-rate is the reaction-rate, and cannot logically be any greater or lesser than it.[18] This leaves a little issue of *which* reaction rate to take: crimes reported? crimes recorded? or crimes successfully prosecuted? Logic can again suggest a resolution. The ultimate 'realist' position (Sellin's) holds that police knowledge of crimes-committed is the closest approximation to the 'real' crime-rate.[19] Thus, conversely, the ultimate 'institutional' position should be based upon the reaction-rate which is *furthest* from, rather than nearest to, the 'realist' conception of the 'offence'. There is another sense in which this is most appropriate, and that is, given that the atheistic attitude to 'crime' embraces the conception that crimes are committed *in* the reaction to (any) acts, and that it denies validity to any conception of the 'dark figure' of crime, because only a court can transform an innocent man into a definitively guilty one, the only reaction which cannot be overturned at a higher level (and thus cannot be part of the 'dark figure') is a legally and permanently established guilty verdict.

The justification for abandoning the 'dark figure' lies in the appreciation that its supposedly realist base in fact contains a fictional 'weasel'. The 'weasel' is apparent (and is emphasised) in the following utilitarian description of the 'dark figure': 'The Dark Figure is to be treated *AS* [it would be] *IF* [it existed]!' Statements with such an open, or concealed 'as if' character were first exposed as useful but consciously false conceptions by Vaihinger (1924). Morris Cohen (1931, p. 492) nicely locates 'fictions' of this sort when he says:

> Fictions appear clearly as assertions that contain an element admittedly false but convenient and even dispensable to bring about certain desired results. Although fictions border on myths which are genuinely believed and on pious frauds which are intended to deceive in aid of good causes, they can be distinguished from them.

Morris Cohen (*ibid.*, pp. 492–3) also comments upon the uses and abuses of such 'fictions' in a way directly applicable to the particular fiction of the 'dark figure':

> From the point of view of social policy fictions are, like eloquence, important in giving emotional drive to propositions that we wish to see accepted. They can be used . . . to keep up a pleasant veneration for truths which [should] have been abandoned. . . . But, if fictions sometimes facilitate change they often hinder it by cultivating undue regard for the past. . . . The interest in truth is in fact not as great as in preservation of

cherised beliefs, even though the latter involves feelings which while temporarily pleasant prove ultimately to be illusions.[20]

So, whither official criminal statistics? The original positivist view was apparently one of dogmatic and almost religious belief in the ability of official criminal statistics to reveal information about criminals. A conventional current positivist tendency is to pay introductory lip-service to the difficulties of bias, selectivity, and so on, but nevertheless blunder on to treat the figures 'as if' the difficulties were merely limiting rather than universal criticisms. It is curious how little the alleged alternative to criminological positivism – the conventional labelling perspective – differs from this position. The lowest common denominator of both current positivist and conventional labelling positions is most neatly summarised as an 'agnostic' attitude towards official criminal statistics: 'crime', like God, is fervently believed in, although its extent (like God's existence) is not held to be wholly knowable.[21] An attitude to official criminal statistics more appropriate to a labelling *theory* (as opposed to a labelling perspective) is a qual- ified 'atheism'.[22] Atheism because of disbelief in the 'dark figure' not merely as unknowable (the agnostic position) but further as non-existent; and qualified in two distinct ways. Firstly, derived from the core proposition of the labelling perspective, the atheist position holds that *everything* can be known about 'crime' from official statistical collations of the constitutive reactions to and of it. In the last instance, this invokes what Biderman and Reiss (1967, p. 2) call the 'ultimate juristic view' of crime:

> A given crime is not validly known to have taken place until a court finds someone guilty of that offence. Only at that point in the process has there been an irrevocable decision as to the evidence regarding the objective facts in relation to their legal significance.[23]

From the atheist position, 'crime' is thus *not* an activity engaged in by an offender, it is one formulated (in court) by others. Similarly, 'criminal activity' is the activity of calling activities crimes. There is no resource available to demonstrate that some 'crime' *is*, after all, 'really' committed by offenders, once the slightest shadow of doubt exists, as it now always does (given that it is at least conceivable that one or more of the 'things' described in section (i) of this chapter may be operating), that the empirical basis of the observation might be an artefact of the *process* (rather than the *object*) of that observation.[24]

The second qualification of the atheist position is derived from Kitsuse and Cicourel (1963, pp. 247–8, emphasis added), who ask:

> Granted that there are *practical* reasons for the use of official statistics, are there any *theoretical* grounds which justify their use, or is this large body of data useless for research in the sociology of deviance?

Their 'institutionalist' position naturally recommends that such statistics can only be used to analyse those (the 'controllers') that they were collected BY, and not those (the 'criminals') they were collected OF. At any one time – or between any two – the official juristic crime-rate can tell us, admittedly and limitedly, how *many* people were successfully prosecuted, but the construction of those statistics is such that no acceptable deductions can be made about the 'motives' or 'intentions' of the accused from them. Thus, the central implication of these conceptual observations is that variations in the official crime-rates are allowable as evidence of *control*-waves: but never of *crime*-waves.[25]

(iii) WILKINS'S AMPLIFICATION MODEL REVISITED

Wilkins's model, as I noticed at the outset, has been variously criticised. Part of the confusion, at least, is traceable to Wilkins's original formulation.[26] However, to those who later made crucial use of the model, especially Erikson,[27] have perpetuated rather than resolved the difficulties. My central and as yet unresolved criticism of Wilkins's model is that it conceals a basic contradiction. On the one hand Wilkins's formulation is, in principle, *theoretically infinite* (there is no provision for anything else but an endless increase in the crime-rate). On the other hand the application of the amplification model to crime conceals the inevitable *empirical* fact that the increase in the crime-rate cannot be accelerated *ad infinitum*, without fairly quickly involving 100 per cent of the population – an empirical barrier through which not even a theory may pass.

So, why does not amplification continue indefinitely? The key to answering this lies initially in the appreciation that the crucial aspect of the Wilkins cycle is that it represents *feedback*, and not just that it amplifies (i.e., has a negative effect).[28] Wilkins's main contribution was to suggest simply that crime and control feedback and mutually influence each other (he refers – 1964, p. 267 – to 'mutual trippings') and perform as a mutual causal system, defined by Maruyama (1963, p. 164) as one wherein, 'the elements within a system influence each other simultaneously or alternatingly'.

Feedback (cybernetically conceived) is not in principle endless, although it is if, as in Wilkins's formulation, it is conceived as having stages connected by a 'loop' – a conception essential to supporting Wilkins's claim that no part of the system has hierarchical causal priority, and that, on the contrary (*ibid.*, p. 88), 'The point of entry into such a system which may result in modification of the loop does not have any significance in terms of the outcome'.[29] Wilkins's singular contribution was to show that, under certain conditions, one type of regenerative feedback could have a negative effect (that possibly well-intentioned but misdirected control would progressively increase, or 'amplify', rather than reduce crime), but the swiftness with which this became the new deviancy theorist's compleat work on mutual causal systems concealed two alternative possibilities. These were, firstly, that regenerative feedback might have a positive effect, and secondly, that degenerative feedback (with positive or negative effect), although unfashionable, might be useful to the understanding of deviance (see Fig. 2.6 on page 31).

Mutual regenerative feedback implies a direct (but unstable) relationship between crime and control. Such 'morphogenesis' (Maruyama's term) can have the negative effect which Wilkins popularised, where more control leads to more crime, but may also have the positive (but similarly direct, and thus also ironic) effect of *less* control producing *less* crime. This hitherto concealed form of morphogenesis (amplification is the other form) I will call deviancy-*attenuation*. The possibility of attenuation may be deduced from Maruyama's original (1963, p. 176) model, part of which is reprinted as Fig. 2.2, on page 26. Taking the positive feedback loop P-M-C-P first (marked as (i) on Fig. 2.2), the relationship between each element is positive. Maruyama (*ibid.*, p. 176) comments:[30]

In the loop P-M-C-P, an increase in the number of people

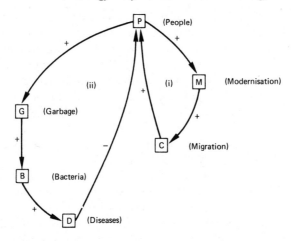

FIG. 2.2 *Maruyama's original model*

causes an increase in modernisation, which in turn increases migration to the city, which in turn increases the number of people in the city [AMPLIFICATION]; on the other hand, a decrease in population causes a decrease in modernisation, which in turn causes a decrease in migration, which in turn decreases population [ATTENUATION].

Accordingly, as the crime-attenuation model is structurally identical to the crime-amplification one, it may be represented (as it is in Fig. 2.3, below) in such a way as to be directly

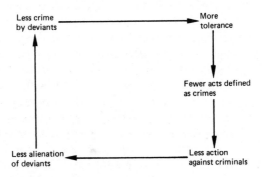

FIG. 2.3 *A 'Wilkins' simple attenuation model*

comparable with Wilkins's single-loop formulation (given in Fig. 2.1 on page 11).

In an attempt to clear up some of the basic confusions, I suggest the (morphogenetic or) deviancy-regeneration models given in Figs. 2.4a, b:

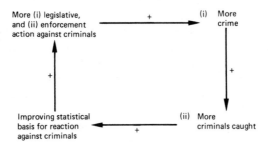

FIG. 2.4a *AMPLIFICATION (vicious circle: negative effect)*[31]

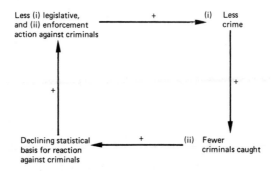

FIG. 2.4b *ATTENUATION (virtuous circle: positive effect)*[32]

However, these formulations only apply to small segments of crime increase, or crime decrease. Regenerative feedback models do not, in themselves, cope with the full range of possible mutual interaction between crime and control. We arrive, here, at the second mutual causal possibility concealed by Wilkins's analysis: the more conventional (and unfashionable) 'morphostasis', or mutual degenerative feedback, where the crime/control relationship is inverse rather than (as with regenerative feedback models) direct. Degenerative feedback morphostasis with a negative effect we may call *expansion*; degenerative feedback morphostasis with a positive effect, we may refer to as *contraction*. Referring again to Maruyama's model (1963, p. 176), partially reprinted as Fig. 2.2, opposite, let us consider loop (ii) P-G-B-D-P. Maruyama (*ibid.*,

p. 177) says:

> Let us take the next loop P-G-B-D-P. This loop contains a
> negative influence from D to P. In this loop, an increase in
> population causes an increase in the amount of garbage per
> area, which in turn causes an increase in the number of bacteria
> per area, which in turn causes an increase in the number of
> diseases, which in turn causes a decrease in population. In
> short, an increase in population causes a decrease in population
> through garbage, bacteria and diseases.... [CONTRAC-
> TION] On the other hand, a decrease in population causes a
> decrease in garbage, bacteria, and diseases, and thus causes an
> increase in population [EXPANSION].

The (morphostatic or) degenerative model is expressed diagrammatically and criminologically in Figs. 2.5a, 2.5b, below.

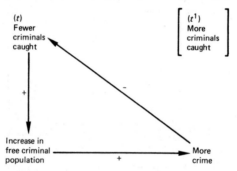

FIG. 2.5a *EXPANSION (negative effect)*
[t = time]

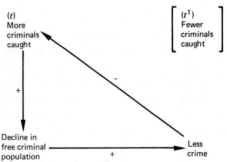

FIG. 2.5b *CONTRACTION (positive effect)*
[t = time]

A curious and hitherto neglected empirical feature of crime-rates appears at this juncture. Both Fig 2.4b (Attenuation) and Fig. 2.5b (Contraction) specify a *reduction* of crime. This is no mere theoretical deduction: examples abound. *Constructed* falls (fewer originally defined non-deviant acts are defined as deviant) originate in legislative or judicial enterprise. As with rises, legislative action is more influential. Gatrell and Hadden (1972, p. 356, emphasis added) report that:

> The Criminal Justice Act of 1855 provided for the summary trial of a much wider range of hitherto indictable larcenies, including all thefts involving property valued at less than five shillings if the accused consented to the summary trial, and all other simple thefts if the accused pleaded guilty. *As soon as the Act took effect it naturally led to an immediate drop in the absolute number of committals for indictable offences against property* from 23,241, 25,677 and 22,347 in 1853, 1854 and 1855 respectively, to 15,928 in 1856. . . . *An equally sudden decrease in both the committal rates and the rates for offences known to the police was caused by the Summary Jurisdiction Act of 1897.* . . . As a result . . . the committal rates for all indictable offences dropped correspondingly from 106.3 to 95.4 of the male population and from 25.0 to 21.4 of the female population.

Judicial moral enterprise may also constructively reduce 'crime'. For example in April 1976 Judge Blomefield ruled at Reading Crown Court that possession of psilocin (an hallucinogen classified as Class A – most dangerous – in the Misuse of Drugs Act, 1971) was not illegal when derived from the common toadstool (*The Times*, 14.4.76), and the Court of Appeal has recently ruled that it is no longer an offence to possess cannabis when derived from any part of the plant other than its 'flowering or fruiting tops' (*Daily Telegraph*, 14.1.77), a decision later confirmed by the House of Lords (*Guardian*, 7.4.78).

Fantasy falls (fewer of those acts originally committed are discovered) have a philosophically infallible proof. Since the acts-which-can-be[-called]-crime are logically represented by that category 'any acts', then a smaller crime-rate must reflect a change in the selection process rather than a decline in the number of acts from which that selection is made. Thus, any fall in the crime-rate can only represent, inasmuch as there have been no constructed or book-keeping changes, a fantasy fall. One example will do. A fantasy fall has gradually occurred in the numbers of arrests both for cannabis offences (a fall from a peak of 11,111 in 1973 to 8837 in 1975) and for LSD-25 convictions (dropping from 1537 in 1971 to just 791 in 1975). The organisation Release, on the other hand, believes that hallucinogen-use is growing, and that the offender rate fall merely represents the liberalisation of police attitudes and the decline in their investigative action.

Thirdly, *book-keeping* falls (fewer originally or subsequently discovered deviant acts are officially collated) have regularly been noticed. Bell (1960a, p. 153), for example, documents how the American crime-rate drops dramatically every 10 years as the crime-rate is dependent on crime statistics which are changed annually, and population totals which are only updated every tenth year. To give another example, the noticed statistical decline in heroin use which occurred in 1969 (down from 2240 in 1968 to 1417 in 1969) is invisibly backed by a concomitant increase in those on the then preferred methadone substitute (N.P.D.S., 1976, p. 8).[33]

Fourthly, *Reporting* falls (less mass media coverage of deviant events) represent a mass media interest in crime which wanes as frequently as it waxes. Young (1971a, pp. 37–8) notices:

> We may chart the course of the great panic over drug abuse which occurred during 1967 by examining the amount of newspaper space devoted to this topic. The number of column inches in *The Times* for the four-week period beginning 29th May was 37; because of the Jagger trial this exploded to 709 in the period beginning 27th June; it continued at a high level of 591 over the next four weeks; and then began to abate from 21st August onwards, when the number of column inches was 107.[34]

As with crime-rate rises, precisely because I have been able to again demonstrate the feasibility of the operation of the other four 'things', no evidence may be adduced to indicate the reality of *Real* falls. However, let me pursue another implication of my argument in the next section: one with particularly far-reaching consequences.

(iv) CONTROL WAVES: A GENERAL MODEL

So far, I have resuscitated assorted snippets of empirical evidence to show that crime-rates usually and periodically fall (as well as rise); recommended that this evidence be viewed as demonstrating the operation of control – and *not* of some separately conceived entity called 'crime'; and regurgitated a facet of cybernetics (i.e., *de*generation) which had been unfortunately neglected when Wilkins applied the principles of mutual causality to the study of crime and control. Wilkins chose merely to draw the attention of criminologists to amplification, thus eliding (as can be seen from Fig. 2.6, below) three-quarters of the potential value of mutual causality analysis.

FEEDBACK TYPE

		(Morphogenesis) Regenerative	(Morphostasis) Degenerative
FEEDBACK EFFECT	Positive	ATTENUATION	CONTRACTION
	Negative	AMPLIFICATION	EXPANSION

FIG. 2.6 *Mutual causality possibilities*

Now, what is particularly interesting about *de*generation as opposed to *re*generation is that these two forms of morphostasis (contraction and expansion) are theoretically and necessarily linked in an alternating cycle. Maruyama (1963, p. 177, emphasis added) refers thus to the degenerative feedback population model: 'In this [degenerative feedback] loop, therefore, any change in population is *counteracted by itself.*'

Thus, contraction *inevitably* breeds expansion, and vice versa. Accordingly, we may consecutively serialise the Expansion and Contraction models, producing a self-repeating morphostasis oscillation (given in Fig. 2.7 on page 32; cf. Figs. 2.5a, 2.5b, on page 28).

So, contraction and expansion are theoretically and logically linked: neither need necessarily occur, but once one does, the other will inevitably follow. Amplification and attenuation, on the other hand, are merely optional possibilities. As options, however, they are restricted. The seeds of attenuation are only found in the detritus of contraction: the impetus for amplification only discoverable in the crest of expansion. On that basis, an optimal

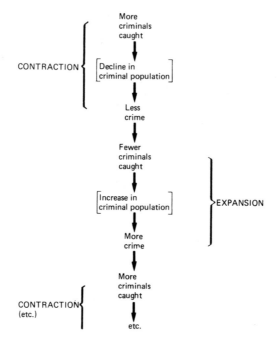

FIG. 2.7 *Positive/negative morphostasis oscillation*

model of a control-wave can be constructed (Fig. 2.8, opposite). The control-wave model has the immediate advantages both of logical rather than metaphysical structure,[35] and of being able to portray analytically what I have shown to be the case empirically (i.e., that evidence of crime-rates shows them to rise and fall). I have diagrammed the model as a four-phase movement, although the attenuation and amplification phases are optional (either may appear separately, or both may appear together in any particular instance). Although the loop sequence must be expansion (amplification) – contraction (attenuation), substantive application might begin at any point.[36]

An abbreviation has crept into the presentation of my analysis roughly here: I use the words 'crime' and 'criminal' in Figs. 2.6 and 2.8, whereas the logic of the preceding argument would seem to specify the use of the words 'act' and 'actors' as replacements. But does it? Looking first at 'crime', I am not suggesting that a greater or fewer number of acts take place – this being undemon-

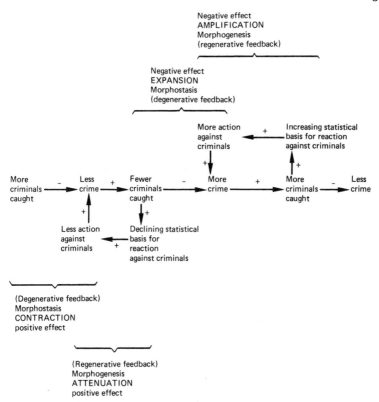

FIG. 2.8 *A general model of control waves*

strable given the force of the argument presented in section (ii) of this chapter. Instead, I am employing an elision based upon the juristic conception of crime (already discussed), and an acknowledgement of the pragmatic basis of control. The latter has been exquisitely analysed by Matza (1969, pp. 180–195) as a form of 'collective representation'. The structural dilemma of policing (*vide* Skolnick, 1966), encased within democratic political expediency, prompts the police to maintain order at the expense of upholding law. [In fact, this invidious propensity has been documented in one of the monographs (Young, 1971) which partly provided the empirical impetus for the theoretical revision of mutual causality envisaged at the beginning of this chapter]. Matza is able to offer a labelling-sensitive version of the 'normal' and the 'criminal' population by demonstrating that neither are objectively or behaviourally identifiable self-sustaining groups, but are, contrarily, 'representations' produced through the mechanisms evoked to solve the procedural law/order dilemma (and provided for in the reactions of others). The chief mechanism is the institution of suspicion, emerging *incidentally* through the (rare) use of the classic investigatory method implemented through detection within the 'normal' population;[37] yet *methodically* through the (more commonly practised) bureaucratic investigatory method implemented through harassment of the 'criminal' population.[38]

Thus, it is the processes of social control which produce and define the 'criminal' population. Matza (*ibid.*, p. 181) continues:

> The main foundation for the institution of suspicion lies in its workability as a tentative solution to the constant pressures to which police are subjected – and not in the existence of inevitable suspects who command or otherwise intimidate an institutional response. Suspects are utilised or employed by a police force as part of the method by which an uneasy accommodation with other elements of state and society is reached. Thus viewed, the institution of suspicion, which focuses attention on a regular but small criminal corps, is mainly based on the police pursuit of other socially valuable goals; taken by itself, the pursuit of thieves could be managed in quite different ways.

It is not, then, a question of whether or not an individual has broken the law (even ultimately juristically defined) which is used to locate him as a member of the 'criminal' population, but rather, it is a matter of whether or not the individual concerned is 'formulated' as 'really' an 'essential' criminal: a production of identity which is inherently tautological.[39] The fruits of that production are clear: a 'criminal' population is assembled in order to account for, stand for and 'collectively represent' 'crime'. This slight digression should counter any critical claim that the energetic basis of Fig. 2.7 (or Fig. 2.8) is mechanistic or behaviouristic. Control produces a corps of 'criminals', and control-waves (which function pragmatically on a basis of 'criminal' actors rather than 'crime' acts) can alternatively overflow and deplete their own capability for control activity. Thus, the size of the 'criminal' population is wholly determined by the exercise and experience of control, with particular members being periodically extruded into or included from the 'normal' population. That is the logical parameter of the control-wave model: in fact, its pragmatic operation is guaranteed by forms of temporary banishment (deportation, or incarceration), which are critical because they contribute to the 'wave' effect of control.[40] More important still (in supporting my position that the *only* variable, in the crime-control equation, is control), this feature is *endogenous* to control. This is rather crucial because it is capable of providing an explanation for the initial problematic: why doesn't amplification (or attenuation) continue indefinitely? This is important enough to warrant a formal answer.

Precisely the same problem is faced in the study of business cycles. There, the endogenous principle of diminishing returns operates to explain why peaks flatten out (why amplification becomes contraction); and the obverse, the principle of increasing returns, is used to account for why troughs bottom-out (why attenuation becomes expansion). Stated more formally, this becomes the *Principle of Deceleration*: The effect of progression is gradually reversed by changing the balance between that subtracted from, and that remaining in a finite supply.

Let me describe the source of the principle: business cycles.[41] As Mitchell (1941, p. 1) puts it, 'the very conditions of business depression beget a revival of activity', and the seeds of depression are just as naturally found in the conditions of prosperity. In business, as an expansion of trade gets under way, relative costs begin to rise (as pools of labour, plant, money and so on begin to diminish, only the dregs of each are left to buttress continued expansion), and eat into profit margins. Production is increased to counter this decline, but eventually production gluts face consumption lags, and prosperity becomes depression. Applied to criminology, this emerges as the Principle of Diminishing (or increasing) 'Criminals'.[42] With my contrololological tongue ever so slightly in my analytic cheek, let me offer a hypothetical example.

Starting (arbitrarily) with a hardening of judicial attitudes, or a tightening of police opinions, a consistent rate of enforcement or detection will reflect this increase and more criminals will be caught.[43] This healthy looking crime expansion may well get caught up in regenerative feedback amplification. The increase in the apprehension rate will provide a sound objective basis for a broad-based attack on increasing 'criminality'. Legislative action may redefine more acts as crimes, thus increasing the potential 'criminal' population. More enforcement action will see to it that more of this population is apprehended, and this provides an even sounder basis for a greater attack on ever-increasing 'criminality'; and so on.

But, sooner or later, at some point in this boom, the Principle of Deceleration (here in the guise of the Law of Diminishing Criminals) must come into effect. Ultimately, the more 'criminals' that are caught, the fewer there are left free to commit 'crimes'. This is an inescapable fact of life.[44] Its effect will gradually increase until the balance between that subtracted from, and that remaining in (or adding to) the finite supply (here, the 'criminal' population) becomes negative.

At this point, a 'crime' contraction 'leads' lagging control into a full-blown crime depression. Looking at the control contraction in detail: initially, if enforcement is effective, the stock of originally committed but concealed 'criminal' acts will become gradually more depleted, and a consistent rate of enforcement will generate a decreasing rate of discovery (a *fantasy*-crime contraction). This begins to erode juridicial concern, and dampen legislative enthusiasm, and support for repressive criminal legislation will diminish (a *constructed*-crime contraction). Additionally, the simple elapse of time alone will subtract 'news' value from continued reports of the same crime. Also, a falling crime rate is not news, and this, if known, will increase deceleration;[45] thus, there will also be a *reporting*-crime contraction.

The reduction in crime, and the subsequent fall-off in control begins to progressively and regeneratively feed back. Crime attenuation may increase the amplitude of the trough. Less legislative action against criminals reduces the size of the population at risk from the criminal law, and reduced enforcement catches (creates) fewer 'criminals'.[46] But irony usually reasserts itself at this point, and the Principle of Deceleration (now as the Principle of Increasing Criminals) comes into play.

Eventually, if fewer members of the criminal population are caught, more are at large (this accelerates as prison sentences expire), and thus the crime-rate will start to recover from its depressed state, and will begin to flourish in a phase of expansion. A constant enforcement rate will (after a suitable lag) begin to reflect this increase, and more criminals will be caught. This healthy expansion may well get caught up in regenerative feedback amplification and, if so, a fresh control wave will start with a vengeance.

Although I have tried to document this argument with a small selection of confirming examples, the grounds of verification of the model are theoretical and logical; and so it should, I suggest, be assessed upon its theoretical merits rather than its putative relevance to particular cases.[47] On the other hand its utility, naturally, depends upon its applicability. Chapter 3 is both the source from which the propositions and models in Chapter 2 were induced, and an exemplary case of the model in operation.

NOTES

1. Crucially, the main differences between the behaviour of American and British opiate addicts (deductively linked to control by, for example, Schur in 1962, and by Lindesmith in 1965) could be explained as a consequence of control and not of the opiate.

2. The amplification thesis also permitted refutation of the 'evil causes evil' fallacy by replacing it with 'good causes evil', and vice versa; and also the possibility that 'very similar conditions may produce entirely different developments' (Maruyama, 1960, pp. 257–8), or, 'small causes big' and vice versa. Further, the ultimate logical verification of the secondary deviation proposal – the discovery of a 'pure case' of secondary deviance (Lemert, 1967, p. 56, claimed that some cases of stuttering could 'be exclusively a process product') – itself depends upon a crude version of amplification (Lemert refers to 'self-defeating deviance' and 'cycles') in its presentation.

3. Cohen (*ibid.*) for example, continues:

   Putting the stages in some context ... raises [another] defect of the amplification type of model, namely, that it is ahistorical. ... Clearly the use of cybernetic language such as feedback and stimuli is too automatic and mechanistic.

   Young (1971, p. 117) has obviated the deterministic overtones by suggesting that the subject might transcend, or 'mollify' the effects of contract by neutralisation, rejection, or avoidance.

4. Laurie Taylor (1971, p. 73) notes one limitation:

   Wilkins's model only deals with one type of deviance and consequently with one type of deviant reaction. His model does not apply to older, more established forms of deviance which 'run on', as it were.

   However, Taylor has merely noticed that controllers and the mass media do not exacerbate *every* form of criminal activity simultaneously. It is *not* possible to demonstrate that *any* criminal activity is immune from all aspects of amplification. Later, Taylor (with Robertson, 1974, p. 117) specifies the conditionally relevant basis for the model; they suggest that the following conditions are necessary for the amplification process to start: development of a conception of privacy, acceptance of an area of minimum visibility wherein deviance will be tolerated, the presence of a third party to initiate control, deviant self-consciousness, the availability of alternative deviant identities, a shared protective ideology, and a group decision to indulge in collective defence.

5. Young (1971, p. 116) comments:

> A common and misplaced criticism of the deviancy amplification approach is that it makes increased deviancy seem inevitable. This is widely off the mark, however, for by showing in what conditions, in terms of which principles, amplification occurs, they illustrate inevitably the circumstances in which the reverse process is generated.

6. Wilkins (1964, pp. 91–2) offers a more complex general model (of double-loop amplification) but with similar difficulties:

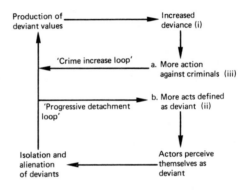

FIG. 2.1a *Wilkins's complex amplification model*

The two processes, the 'crime increase loop' (denoting amplification), and the 'progressive detachment loop' (fantasy translation) (more on the latter in Chapter 3, especially in note 26) are muddled in Wilkins's formulation, and this has bred confusion in Young (1971, 1971a), Armstrong and Wilson (1973, p. 82), and Damer (1974, p. 197).

Although Wilkins uses the word 'positive' to describe feedback here, I shall abandon this formulation (in line with a hitherto ignored suggestion from Maruyama, 1960, p. 260) in favour of the term 'regenerative' (or morphogenesis) when the direction of feedback is the same as the direction of the process within which it is inserted; and 'degenerative' (or morphostasis) when the direction of feedback is opposite to the direction of the process within which it is inserted. This leaves the term 'positive' to apply to those (degenerative or regenerative) occasions when the outcome is in line with the controllers' intentions, and 'negative' when they are not. Confusion here mars Scheff's (1966) otherwise critical contribution to the area: he refers initially (pp. 13–14) to a degenerative overall system (i.e. thermostatic equilibrium maintenance) with an unspecified effect, although later (with his theory of Stable Mental Disorder) perversely attaches an *unstable* regenerative feature to it.

7. The publication of official criminal statistics in England and Wales is variously felt to begin in the first half of the nineteenth century – the exact date depending upon whether one wishes to base the origin on the first prison returns of 1810 (Wiles, 1971, p. 176), or on the earliest comprehensive returns published in 1857 (Morrison, 1897, p. 1). Interpretative difficulties were noticed as early as 1836 by Bulwar (quoted in McClintock, 1970, p. 9), and only three years later, in England, Rawson W. Rawson (1839, p. 320) was able to claim:

> The criminal law of England is at present in a state of transition, and is every year undergoing great changes . . . [i]t must also be borne in mind that the most complete record of the number of criminals arrested does not exhibit the amount of crime committed, as the former depends, in a great measure, upon the disposition of the injured parties or the public to prosecute, and the efficiency of the system of police.

8. For an exquisite example, compare Morrison (1892) with Du Cane (1893).

9. Traffic offences in the Shetland Islands rose by more than 400 per cent in 1977: from 500 in 1976 to a grim 2210. It is all because Mr McKnight won a contract to move some rubble, and his unlicensed lorry crossed a public highway at one point. A diligent law enforcement officer calculated how many times the lorry crossed the road per day, multiplied it by the number of days Mr McKnight had been on the contract, and attempted (unsuccessfully) to deliver 1380 identical summonses [*Sunday Times*, 23.2.78].

10. Beattie (1974, p. 83, fn. 76) shows how the massive increase in petty larceny cases in 18th-century England was due to sympathetic court clerks who defined most property thefts (even one theft of eleven half-crowns, or £1.37½p.) as 'petty larceny' (allegedly theft of items worth 10d., or 5p., and below) in order to spare convicted offenders the otherwise mandatory death penalty. Gatrell and Hadden (1972, p. 356) describe how the repeal of those capital statutes in the early 19th century produced a phenomenal rise in the rate of indictable committals from 1814 to 1819.

11. Judge Roderick Smith rapped Northumbria police for abusing the system where an offender appears in court and has other offences considered. When a 17-year-old youth appeared before him, the judge was asked to take 31 other offences into consideration, after the youth had been convicted of taking a car without consent. The youth's counsel said the other offences were nearly all for trying to take cars. Judge Smith said: 'A lad tries to get into 50 different cars, gets into the fifty-first, appears charged with taking it and 50 other offences to be taken into consideration. *All it can be thought to be doing is to improve the detection rate of the Northumbria Constabulary.* It is an abuse of the system whereby other offences are taken into consideration. I keep on saying it – no one takes the slightest notice of what I say. Except in this case – these 31 offences will not be taken into consideration'. Mr Barry Price, Assistant Chief Constable (Crime and Operations), Northumbria Police, said today *they abided 'to the letter' with strict accounting rules laid down by the Home Office. [Evening Chronicle*, 5.2.77.] (Drawn to my attention by Bob Roshier, emphasis added.)

12. The arch reification of these feet of clay is the F.B.I. crime-clock. Megaree (1977, p. 18) tells us:

> Every three seconds a light blinks under a large clock in the lobby of the J. Edgar Hoover Building in Washington, D.C. According to official FBI statistics, this signifies that somewhere in the United States a serious crime has taken place. The light blinks day and night, 19 times a minute, 1140 times an hour, 27360 times a day. At the end of the year, when new crime statistics have been collected, the clock is stopped and reprogrammed to blink at a faster rate. In the 15-year period from 1960 through 1975, the blinking light was speeded up by 203 percent.

13. See, for example, the decision to separately display 'mugging' offences in the official criminal statistics (there is no such offence as 'mugging') as a response to the vitriolic media campaign of the early 1970s: a campaign superbly documented in Hall *et al.* (1978). Further, Thompson (1975a, p. 263) reports how blackmailers get some of their ideas from the published exploits of others, and Bell (1960a, p. 154) and Mackay (1852, p. 41) offer a similar analysis of 'epidemics' of kidnapping and poisoning.

14. The reason why the institutional programme of Kitsuse and Cicourel has never been fully taken up (until now) is that whilst its logical implications were impeccable, they were not (then) deemed also important. At the time (see e.g., Cohen, 1974) it was apparently felt more important to co-opt the myth of the dark figure in order to invalidate the distinction (which positivist criminology depends upon) between 'control' and 'sample' populations.

15. Max Atkinson is the only sociologist to accept the unqualified critique of official statistics (see his Ch. 3 in Atkinson, 1978), and to do analysis of phenomena on the basis of a logical extension of that position (see Atkinson, 1971).

16. The 'dark figure' in criminology plays a role identical to that played by the 'silent majority' in politics. Hugo Young has said of the latter (*Sunday Times* n.d. [1972?] emphasis added) [the reader may wish to exchange 'dark' for silent, 'figure' for majority, and 'criminologist' for politician, etc., in the following quotation]:

> For silence is what gives the silent majority its special attraction to a politician – silence is the source of its unassailable authenticity. It proposes no arguments which might be exposed, no tangible expressions . . . which might be vulnerable to dispute. He who speaks for the silent majority offers something much more attractive than mere argument, namely initiation into secrets which he alone has divined. The natural dramatic power of the voice hitherto unheard, the opinion hitherto modestly withheld, is infinitely magnified when it is alleged to be the unrevealed opinion of several million citizens.
>
> Through these privileged spokesmen, who are gifted with telepathic powers, the silent majority discloses itself . . . [but] the silent majority is not, as is supposed, the embodiment of some more perfect democratic will. It is, on the contrary, profoundly undemocratic. . . . *It has been invented for a single purpose: to clothe with a spurious respectability minority prejudices which lack the support of rational argument.*

17. Naturally, intent is not a legal consideration with strict liability offences (see Carson, 1970), although these cases are *not* crimes until the evidence of their behavioural occurrence has been accepted as fact in a court of law.

18. Thus it is equally positivistic to assert that there might be a 'dark figure' of *control* (i.e., to cater for the allegedly 'falsely accused'). We have no democratic resource available to point out false accusations other than court decisions. An established guilty verdict found in a court of law cannot logically (or legally) be erroneous.

19. Sellin's rule (quoted in Ferracuti, Hernandez and Wolfgang, 1962, p. 114) is that: 'The value of criminal statistics as the basis for the measurement of criminality in geographic areas decreases as the procedure takes us further away from the offence itself'. The Sellin view is, correspondingly, that police knowledge of crimes-committed (for which there may not be a known offender) is the closest approximation to the real crime-rate. Coleman and Bottomley (1976, p. 345) point out, however, that apart from its juristic limitations, 'with one or two exceptions, "crime" for the police means those offences for which crime complaint and crime report forms have to be completed'.

20. In particular, according to Vaihinger (1924, p. 34), the 'dark figure' is a *juristic* fiction; one where 'something that has not happened is regarded as having happened.' I should point out that both 'crime' and 'control' are *summational* fictions. Vaihinger (1924, p. 211) comments that in such a case:

> We are making use of an auxiliary concept, as though this summation were something outside of and apart from the attributes, just as if a genus were thought of as something outside of and apart from the multiplicity of the particular things of which it is formed . . . [thus, such concepts are] . . . nothing but summational expressions for a series of interconnected phenomena and interconnected processes.

21. With agnosticism defined (Webster's *New International Dictionary*, Bell & Sons, London, 1941; Vol. 1: p. 50) as: [and here substitute 'crime' for God] 'The doctrine that neither the existence nor the nature of God . . . is known or knowable. . . . Any doctrine which, while professing belief in God's existence, denies to a greater or lesser extent the knowableness of his nature'. [Cf. Box (1971, pp. 68–9) quoted on p. 18 above]. The use and definition employed here of agnosticism differs from that used by Hindess (1973, p. 11) – a use heavily criticised by Cicourel (in the new Introduction in the 1976 edn. of Cicourel, 1968).

22. The atheistic view of criminal statistics is not necessarily *nihilistic*. But neither is the commonplace criticism that these statistics are biased, incomplete, etc., necessarily *radical*. In fact even vigorous application of the juristic view of crime does not rule out the establishment of a set of statistics which would, firstly, avoid the universal criticisms I have made of conventional statistics (although, of course, still be subject to the limited criticisms of incompleteness and so on); and secondly, provide a platform for a radical critique which is simultaneously constructive. In 1965 Wilkins (1965, p. 282, emphasis added) suggested:

> The proposal to measure 'crime' by means of social cost factors involves a

change of base from 'what the offender tried to do' (intent) to what was the *effect* of his actions. This approach avoids many administrative (as distinct from philosophical) difficulties. The matter of intent is important in moral issues, but morals and social costs are not the same thing and should be separated in the statistics. The two concepts of *what happened* and *what was intended should happen* should not be confounded in one figure which serves to illuminate neither the social nor the ethical matters.

By adopting the 'what happened' criteria exclusively, we might drop (and aid the decriminalisation of) Schur's 'crimes without victims', perhaps include Wilkins's earlier (1963) category of 'crimes without criminals' (referring to losses sustained without being able to attach liability to the architect), and, importantly, elect to consideration that massive category (suggested in a personal communication from Philip Corrigan) of 'victims without crimes' – the unfortunate ingestors of maiming wonder-drugs, passengers on lethal aircraft, operators of dangerous industrial machinery, purchasers of contaminated food, and so on.

23. Naturally, the point of irrevocability assumes that appeals (against verdict) have been unsuccessfully heard. Morrison (1897, p. 7) reached a similar conclusion ('until an offence has been submitted to the judgement of a properly constituted tribunal it is impossible to say in what the offence has consisted, or whether an offence of a criminal character has been committed at all'); however he viewed the court as a way of *measuring* rather than a process of *creating* crime. It is important to establish that sociologists (or/as laymen) can have no warrant to isolate the category 'criminal' without recourse to the definitive judgement of a court in each and every case (within which, although we might not agree with the verdict, it has been 'established' for all societal practical purposes). To alternatively believe that the court can be challenged as to the correctness of its classification invokes an interminably positivistic *correspondence* theory upon the basis of that challenge which itself employs a *convergence* epistemological base. As Atkinson (1978, p. 194) puts it:

> The correctness of a description cannot be established in any once and for all 'objective' way so long as two persons can point to a third person and apply different descriptors.

24. As even Gatrell and Hadden (1972, p. 377, emphasis added) put it:

> We may be justified in concluding that a decrease in property crime in the long-term would in some way be related to an overall increase in prosperity. *But this must be argued chiefly on a priori grounds, since there is no statistical method by which the effects of this factor can be distinguished from the effects of police and court developments.*

25. This position naturally has certain implications for those sociological and historical studies which base their analysis and conclusions upon official statistics. An ironic suggestion originally offered by von Hentig and translated by Vold (1958, p. 168) is nicely appropriate here:

> As information becomes more specific and accurate so that comparisons can be made more explicit, the simple correlation that seemed so obvious

from the analysis of more crude data with less refined methods is no longer so evident. In this way, von Mayr's 1867 rule (taken from the analysis of Bavaria in 1836–61) that, 'for every half-penny increase in the price of rye there would be an increase of one theft per 100,000 persons', and vice versa, has been progressively qualified.

Thus, although early studies were able to positively establish an inverse correlation between theft and economic conditions (e.g., as did von Mayr), or positively disestablish one (e.g., as did Mayhew and Biney, 1862, p. 450) – depending chiefly upon the analysts' preconceptions [this reached a ludicrous extreme when Du Cane (1893) re-examined data previously analysed by Morrison (1892) and produced opposite conclusions], increasing statistical sophistication has improved the power of the analyst to bend the data to fit any theory. In this way, Thomas's (1927) idea of a 'lag' effectively means that *any* original correlation can be 'lagged' to produce the desired inverse relationship. An illusory conceptual sophistication is also present in many of the better historical studies. Phelps (1929), Radzinowicz (1941, 1941a), Hobbs (1943), Short (1952), Beattie (1972; 1974), Zehr (1976), Hanawalt (1974), Samaha (1974), Gatrell and Hadden (1972) and Philips (1977) all mention the various biases (*constructed, fantasy, book-keeping, reporting*) that I have discussed, but erroneously conceive of them as limiting rather than universal criticisms: positivistically as quantifiable factors to be taken into consideration when 'weighting' the evidence. Behind this fallacy lies the belief that the extent of the distortion they produce is in principle knowable, and only currently unobtainable due to the present inadequacy of statistical cleaning techniques. The possibility of a correlation *at all* has been ably criticised by Thompson (1971, p. 78) as 'spasmodic determinism', and aptly by Linebaugh (1975, p. 100) as 'mechanical positivism'.

26. Wilkins's formulation is ambiguous chiefly because he fails to treat the two forms of controller (enforcer and legislator), or the two *types* of audience (police and citizen) as distinct; and because he does not satisfactorily distinguish the actions and feelings of the controllers from the actions and feelings of the controlled. Instead, I shall consider the actions and feelings of the controll*ers* (and only the actions of the controll*ed* when relevant).

27. Erikson (1966) offers little help in resolving the confusions noticed here in Wilkins's scheme. Firstly, his definition of 'crime-waves' (p. 69) is as vague as Wilkins's formulation: it starts by referring to a *constructed* rise ('the community begins to censure forms of behaviour which have been present in the group for some time but have never attracted any particular attention before'), moves to a *real*-rise ('certain people in the group who have already acquired a disposition to act deviantly move into the breach and begin to test the boundary in question') and ends with a mere *reporting*-rise ('"crime waves" refer to a rash of publicity'). Secondly, his account of the origin of crime-waves, the 'boundary crisis' (sparked off, p. 68, 'wherever a community is confronted by a significant relocation of boundaries, a shift in its territorial position, it is likely to experience a change in the kinds of behaviour handled by its various agencies of control') is ultimately teleological in its putative reliance on members to fill the posited 'breach' (see Roshier, 1977, for a masterly critique of the implied 'functions of crime' argument). Thirdly, Erikson's empirical examples of waves differ in type.

The 'convulsive episode' which he called the Antinomian controversy is a *constructed*-rise, the Quaker invasion was a *constructed* leading to an allegedly *real* increase; and the witches of Salem episode was described as a *real*-rise. Fourthly, Erikson has only a vague *ad hoc* theory of the decline of such episodes. In the last case, he merely claims (p. 149) 'the whole witchcraft mania began to fade', or (p. 152), an almost Churchillian 'the tide had begun to turn'. Finally, his resolution of the apparent disparity between the functional uniformity of crime-rates (see Durkheim's *Suicide*) and the boundary-maintaining quality of waves in the crime-rate (see Durkheim's *Division of Labour*) is a pure artefact of his data. Erikson's resolution of the contradiction is to claim that whilst the number of *offences* rises, the number of *deviants* stays the same. A glance at the book's appendices shows that the proof of this is controversial. Because the Puritans did not observe consistent rules of spelling, and because consecutive generations preserved the same christian name, counting the number of offenders was a mistake-prone process. Further, estimates of overall populations were on Erikson's own admission 'precarious' and sometimes replaced by sheer guesswork. As well as this, Erikson unreservedly makes the claim that the available agencies of social control exhausted all crimes actually committed. He bases this claim upon the *triviality* of many cases coming before the Essex County Court (see note 25 above), on the assumption that these would normally be the last cases to concern the court, and that their presence therefore demonstrates that all the serious cases were also tried, and upon the excessive *intolerance* of community labellers. The last point depends upon the view that the private stock of deviant acts will be quicker exhausted by greater vigilance and less tolerance. One might alternatively suggest that intolerance or vigilance would merely 'create' *more* deviant acts. In other words, that amplification might occur.

28. Noble (1977, p. 115) defines negative feedback as an occasion when 'some of the output of the system is *subtracted* from the input and thus fed back into the system', and positive feedback as, '*adding* some of the output to the input'. This is a clear formulation, but most accounts are very confused. Unravelling this confusion requires separating some understandable analogical muddles. The idea of amplification derives from an analogy with electronics (for example, a hearing-aid lapses into regenerative feedback when it malfunctions, i.e., has a negative effect – see: Wender, 1968, p. 310), which was used as a figure to illustrate the more complex analogical base of the servo-mechanism (the thermostat positive effect/degenerative feedback model – Van Doorn, 1975, pp. 11–13) where it was clear that it was degenerative feedback and not just amplification at work. Unfortunately, the ecological example (the regenerative feedback/negative effect case of the rock which progressively becomes dust through accelerating frost-shattering (Wender, 1968, pp. 3, 9–10), and the interactional special case (the double mirror problem as exemplified in the writings of Cooley, 1902, and Laing *et al.*, 1966), have confused the situation and made infinite amplification (incorrectly conceived as a spiral) appear as the norm. Whereas in fact, in most of the original bases of the model, 'saturation' of some sort occurs. Noble (1977, p. 116) points out that for the electronic example 'the howl does not grow louder for ever – it "saturates" or reaches a maximum

intensity which is finite. This is because the ability of the amplifier to convert electrical energy is limited'. I shall show that a similar 'saturation' occurs, too, in the social world.

29. Maruyama (1963, p. 177) defines 'loop' as a circuit wherein: 'each element has an influence on all other elements either directly or indirectly, and each element influences itself through other elements'.

30. The 'sign' of the feedback (i.e., regenerative) is the same (regenerative) as long as there are no degenerative links (*or*, an even number of degenerative links) in the loop.

31. Lemert's (1967, p. 198) progressive exclusion model is a nice example of this; as are Scheff's two examples (1966, pp. 97, 99) of the regenerative link between stigmatisation and withdrawal amongst the mentally ill.

32. To parallel Lemert (see last note) we might imagine love (as a context of inclusion) as a good example of regenerative attenuation.

33. Wilkins (1963, p. 329) notes:

> Between the years 1954 and 1955 the offence of malicious damage to property dropped from 5156 to 2123. It is perhaps sufficiently obvious that the sudden drop in this category of offences is due to changes in the system of recording these offences.

Center and Smith (1973, p. 1058, fn. 55) further note:

> The President's Commission on Crime in the District of Colombia found that slight changes in classification guidelines resulted in a great change in certain crime categories. As far as aggravated assault was concerned, for example, 'revision of the classification rules in the District of Colombia . . . resulted in a drop from 4558 aggravated assaults in 1955 to 2824 in 1956, a decline of 40 per cent'.

34. See Potter (1926, pp. 14–17) for another good example of a reporting fall.

35. Hitherto, it has been conveniently forgotten that protestations about the incidence of crime-waves *logically* demand that crime not only rise to a peak, but later fall into a trough. Such are waves. For some empirical evidence of this, see Potter (1926). Both Silver (1967, p. 2) and Conklin (1975) have pointed up the consequent lay fallacy in the usual social construction of criminal history which depicts crime-waves as eternally running upon an ever escalating spot. Douglas (1971, p. 100) describes the 'atheistic' attitude to crime-waves thus:

> We can expect that the official rates will continue to rise steadily for many years to come, but it would be a mistake to believe that this has anything to do with what criminals or other forms of deviants are doing.

[Crime] waves are thus control [waves]. Further, it is noteworthy to recall that the application of the wave metaphor to criminal activity in fact presupposes a form of theorising about crime itself. Although the use of waves is now cunningly metaphoric, it is nevertheless based upon a history of original literal meaning. Then, crime was felt to be a disease, and accordingly, felt to naturally appear in epidemics (see note 45 below). For example (Anon. 1863, p. 79):

Crimes, like some other diseases, are often epidemical. They appear from time to time in new forms and in strangely gathered force, rage awhile, and then die away.

At least this implied the occasional trough – later conveniently forgotten. It took Potter (1926, p. 13) to offer an analogy based on water but including the vital elements of trough alternation with crest, and overall precipitation by controllers. She says (*ibid.*):

> Instead of an engulfing wave, we shall more accurately visualise the situation if we liken it to the mechanically driven fountain, the waters of which are ejected only to fall back into the basin to be repumped into the air once more.

Thus, whilst the 'figure' which we may now conjure up in using the wave metaphor for crime is that of periodically activated masses of criminals protected from destroying the shifting sands of decency and righteousness only by the stubborn and constant breakwaters of social control, such continued and uncritical use of the usual metaphor *implies* that crime is pathological, and control normal.

36. The rise and fall of successive waves of fashionable working-class juvenile resistance, which Cohen (1973, p. 180) calls 'expressive fringe delinquency' (Teddy boys, Mods and Rockers, Skinheads, Hell's Angels) exemplify this pattern. However, as I have already suggested, the straightforward discussion of moral 'panics' (amplification) leaves understanding of 'pre-panics' (expansion), 'un-panics' (contraction) and possible 'anti-panics' (attenuation) to the empirical and *ad hoc* imagination. But it is not more empirical work which is needed, but rather an improved theoretical model upon which *existing* empirical observations may be hung. *That* is the warrant for the control-wave model.

37. Matza (1969, pp. 184, 185) claims:

> Everybody is subjected to incidental suspicion – the suspicion which flows from an incident of apparent dereliction. For purposes of argument, it could even be granted that the police encounter and treat incidental aspects more or less even-handedly . . . [e.g.] while not a murderer, I can be suspected, briefly at least, of murder if, incidentally, I should happen to possess hypothetical motive or access to an actual corpse. . . . In homicide, governed partly as it is by the classic modes of detection, possessing motive and access to a corpse is sufficient to excite incidental suspicion. Being known to the deceased *is* the incident.

38. Whereas *everybody* is subjected to (occasional) incidental suspicion (see last note) – thus constituting the 'normal' population – only a *few*, numerically, call (regular) methodical suspicion upon themselves by virtue of their attributed (or self-defined) identity as 'real' criminals, in the process becoming, for all intents and purposes, the 'criminal' population. Matza (1969, pp. 186–7) tells us:

> On the one side, police are pushed toward the method of suspicion by the unquestioningly accurate anticipation that an application of the classic method of detection would elicit a howl of unprecedented volume from

good citizens who know their rights and have the wherewithal to enforce
them; on the other side, police are pressured toward the very same method
by the extension of techniques of cost-accounting and efficiency to their
domain – as reasonable a development, probably, as their extension to
any one of a dozen other public services. It is for this second reason that
the method of suspicion may be termed bureaucratic.

39. The latter depends upon the quality and extent of apprehension. Matza
(*ibid.*, pp. 180, 181) says:

> Apprehended by himself in the full philosophical sense, no longer simply
> one who has been bureaucratically apprehended, the subject has become
> suited for collective representation. The thief will stand for theft. . . . The
> essential thief is employed as a regular suspect . . . the essential thief
> begins his career as an employee of the state. A suspect, he now works for
> the state.

The question of quite *how* members are 'formulated' as having-been-all-
along, and forever-in-the-future 'criminals' is examined and explained in
Ch. 2 of my *Insiders* [Ditton (forthcoming) 1980]. It is sufficient here to
indicate that it is *not* simply an issue of the type of suspicion invoked, nor the
type of crime involved.

40. A potential empirical point is that control-waves may grow or shrink in
amplitude, with successive cycles being either 'damped' (in times of legislative and enforcement liberalism), or 'explosive' (Rau, 1974, p. 17), as they
are in times of legislative or enforcement conservatism. A more conceptually
resolvable difficulty – the time lag – was originally introduced by Maruyama
(1963, p. 177):

> Such a [degenerative feedback] process may result in *stabilisation* or
> *oscillation*, depending on the time lag involved in the counteraction and the
> size of the counteraction.

Control generally 'lags' crime – however misplaced the perception of the
latter may be (see, for example, Dickson, 1968–9: fn. 33, p. 153). To
consider a sharply relevant *medical* problem, Hughes *et al.* (1972), in an
excellent article, have traced the peaking of heroin use in Chicago between
1949 and 1950 as a *real*-rise peaking in 1949, but with *reported*-crime peaking
in 1950, and with *constructed*-rises (in the form of new legislation) occurring in
1951, 1953, 1954, and 1957. Arrests (*fantasy*-rise) rose dramatically in
1953–8. Thus, in line with current understanding of heroin use (Hunt and
Chambers, 1976), street heroin use suffered a short sharp *real*-rise *and fall*. As
Hughes *et al.* (1972, p. 999) put it, 'In the initial or contagious phase, heroin
spread rapidly. The epidemic quickly reached a peak and was already
declining when the community was finally mobilised to control it'. There is
some evidence, more generally, for the cycle. Thomas (1927, p. 135) notes,
'Whatever the ultimate cause of crime, it is quite apparent, from observation
of any series representing an index of crime from year to year, that it is
subject to fairly wide fluctuations, and tends to increase and decrease in
oscillations'. Hunt and Chambers claim that a common pattern is for heroin
to be introduced into a community by an outsider, and spread within it by

his inside contacts. However, the subsequent epidemic begins to peak rather rapidly, and then decline sharply as secondary distributors fail to continuously discover an increasing number of new friends. Whilst heroin use *prevalence* may persist (and act as a ghost-reality for increasing control) *incidence* declines because (Hunt and Chambers, 1976, p. 17): 'natural populations, including these susceptible to heroin use, are finite'; and (p. 26) 'New heroin use always dies out spontaneously, either by the exposure of all susceptibles or because initiators did not penetrate all the susceptible community'. I have recalled the spurned idea of a *real* movement in this note (it is partly legitimated by the medical rather than criminological basis of the phenomena in question) to make a simple analogical point not about crime-waves but about control lags. Campbell and Ross (1968), Glass (1968), and Ross *et al.* (1970) have demonstrated the perils of simple deduction of this sort when social (crime) rather than natural (medical) phenomena are involved.

41. Mitchell (1941, pp. 61–2) adds:

> The very conditions that make business profitable gradually evolve conditions that threaten a reduction of profits. When the increase in business, at first a cause and later both a cause and a consequence of rising profits, taxes the productive capacity of the existing industrial equipment, the early decline of supplementary costs per unit of output comes gradually to a standstill. Meanwhile, the expectation of making satisfactory profits induces active bidding among enterprises for materials, labor, and loan funds, and sends up their prices. At the same time, the poorer parts of the industrial equipment are brought back to use, the efficiency of labor declines, the incidental wastes of management rise. Thus the prime costs of doing business become heavier. After these processes have been running cumulatively for a while, it becomes difficult to advance selling prices fast enough to avoid a reduction of profits by the encroachment of costs. In many industries the increase in industrial equipment has been so rapid that the full output can scarcely be marketed at the high prices that must be asked. In the trades engaged in construction work new contracts decline when the risk in long-term interest discourages borrowing, and when the cost of construction becomes excessive in the eyes of investors. The decline in bank reserves ultimately makes the banks disinclined to expand loans further – which diminishes the ability of many enterprises to buy as freely as they had planned. The high discount rates also clog the effort to forestall a decline in prices by holding stocks of commodities off the market.

42. Strangely, the currently discredited original pseudo-medical metaphor adopted to explain the rise *and* fall of events and interest in them *could* endogenously cope with its own demise. For example, the witches of Salem (Erikson, 1966, p. 142) were sufficiently powerful to make young girls, 'scream unaccountably, fall into grotesque convulsions, and sometimes scamper along on their hands and knees making noises like the barking of a dog'. A more modern example would be the outburst of 'trembling sickness' and 'hysterical spasms' in a Louisiana high school (a number of school girls were suddenly seized with involuntary convulsive jerking in various parts of their anatomy) reported by Schuler and Parenton (1943), or some previous

examples cited by them – in a footnote (*ibid.*, fn. 1, p. 221) they remind us to:

> See J. F. C. Hecker's book, *Die Tanzswuth, eine Volkskrankheit in Mittelalter. Nach dem Quellen für Aerzte und gebildete Nichtärzte bearbeitet* (Berlin, 1832, subsequently translated into several languages), in which he cites the case of an epidemic occurring in a very large convent in France where a nun started to mew like a cat. In a short while other nuns began to imitate the 'mewing nun' until finally all the nuns met together regularly every day and mewed for several hours (*op. cit.* p. 47). Another case mentioned by Hecker (derived from *Zimmerman on Solitude*, Vol II, Leipzig, 1784) deals with the 'nun-biting' mania of the fifteenth century. 'A nun in a German nunnery fell to biting all her companions. In the course of a short time all the nuns of this convent began biting each other. The news of this infatuation among the nuns soon spread, and passed from convent to convent throughout a greater part of Germany, principally Saxony and Brandenburg. It afterwards visited the nunneries of Holland, and at last the nuns had the biting-mania even in Rome'.

Now, the methodological advantage of encapsulating these events as near-medically epidemic is that the rise and fall of the event is explicable: once attacked, individuals recover (although more other individuals may be afflicted during the expansion phase); gradually, more of the population is being inoculated than still lies at risk. Thus the improving balance between those removed from (inoculated) and those remaining in the finite population provides the impetus for cessation.

43. It is certainly unnecessary for any 'crimes' to have been 'committed' before the reaction sets in. The mugging crime-wave experienced in England in the 1970s was, in fact, a pure control-wave. Hall *et al.* (1978, pp. 183–4) comment: 'there appears to be a vigorous reaction to "mugging" as a socio-criminal phenomenon before there are any actual "muggings" to react to'.

44. An inescapable fact of *logical* life. Naturally, it is obvious that in practice, control-waves do *not* reach the stage of exhausting the pool of possible recruits (the 'normal' population) into the 'criminal' population. However, pragmatically, the pool of possible recruits is generally manufactured to fit control demands. Hall *et al.* (1978, p. 40) refer to this as a 'focused police response', and Gill (1976, pp. 328–30) provides another example of just how pragmatically limited the 'normal' population is on most control occasions.

45. In those cases where crime-reporting suddenly reaches 'epidemic' proportions (Johnson, 1945; Cantril, 1952; Medalia and Larsen, 1958; and Jacobs, 1964), the cessation of such reports is equally swift and sudden. Johnson (1945) investigating the 'phantom anesthetist' of Mattoon considered that (p. 186) 'such outbursts *are necessarily self-limiting*. The bizarre details which captured the public imagination at the beginning of the episode became rather ridiculous when studied more leisurely' (my emphasis). Johnson suggests that an initial wave of hyper-suggestibility is swiftly followed by a wave of contra-suggestibility, but the status of the word 'necessarily' is unclear. Although he appears to mean endogenous, his explanation (leisurely study) relies upon exogenous factors. Cantril (1952, pp. 204–5), by implication at least, locates this alternation as general. In his study of the

effects of Orson Wells's radio transmission of an unframed version of H. G. Wells's *Invasion from Mars*, Cantril reports that the conditions of suggestibility (lack of knowledge of the event) are simultaneously the conditions of counter-suggestibility (the motivation for increased knowledge). Medalia and Larsen (1958), studying the Seattle windshield pitting epidemic, disagree with Johnson and claim (quite rightly) that the claim of reappearing rationality in the leisurely consideration of events is both unnecessary and unlikely. In fact, the *belief* in delusions may persist even after *interest* in them wanes (cf. the extended period of hysteria and suggestibility to reports of flying saucers as documented by Buckner, 1968). However, Jacobs's careful study of the 'phantom slasher' of Taipei strongly supports the idea of feedback of hysteria and suggestibility ('the actual infliction of the wounds under alleged mysterious circumstances by allegedly mysterious individuals acting-out of allegedly mysterious motives were both a product of, and helped to further intensify, the hyper-suggestibility so characteristic of the affair', p. 326) although he lays the rapid deceleration of the affair at the door of an empirically *ad hoc* conspiracy between newspaper owners and the 'authorities'.

46. Some crimes may naturally expire at this point. Unlike unrestrained amplification (which approaches infinity) which is technically inconceivable, endless attenuation (which approaches zero) *is* technically possible. (*Vide* the demise of such fanciful 19th-century criminal types as the 'deal lurker', as chronicled by Mayhew, 1862, Vol IV, p. 25).

47. Although my criticism of official statistics was severe, I believe that (with Seidman and Couzens, 1974, p. 461) 'knowledge of our ignorance is better than the error to which use of [criminal] statistics may lead'. It is at least worth appreciating (with Quinney 1975, p. 109) that 'in the final analysis crime rates have to be understood as political devices'.

3 'Mr Big' and 'The Godfather': Shoppers, Dealers and Squealers as Dramatic Characters in a Factory Control Wave

DRAMATIS PERSONAE

Wally	Despatch Manager
Keith	Despatch chargehands
Donald	
Doug Philips (b)	
Basil	
Geoff	
Larry	Despatch operatives
Barney	
Jim	
Rob Siddell (s)	
Fatty Siddell (f)	Head cleaner
Alfred	Garage employee
Billy Grimes (s)	Garage foreman
Cyril Grimes (f)	Head storeman
George	
Lonny	
Bert	Wholesale salesmen
Claude	
Mr Eadley	Bakery Manager
Mr Morrisey	Night Manager
Mr Smarteagh	Managing Director
Themselves	2 H.Q. Security men
Dan Philips (b)	Despatch chargehand ('retired')

(b) brother   (s) son   (f) father

(i) INTRODUCTION: A CASE STUDY IN CONTROLOLOGY

In the 17-month period stretching between the beginning of August 1971 and the end of May 1973, I worked a total of nearly seven months simultaneously as a despatch operative at the Wellbread Bakery, and as a participant observer from the University of Durham.[1] Participant observation data was backed by intensive, unstructured and tape-recorded interviews with all the despatch staff. These interviews were conducted after the bulk of the participant observation data had been collected.[2] As a whole, this period of research was sandwiched between some participant observation in the production department (reported in Ditton, 1972, 1972a, and 1976), and some later work as a bread salesman (reported in great detail in Ditton, 1977).

I had intended to work as a despatch operative to throw some comparative light on workers' experiences of boredom (a problem which had particularly irritated the plant men), but always with an eye to any problem which the despatch men might perceive as especially germane to their work experience. In the event, in the despatch department, the problem of boredom turned out to be totally eclipsed by a far more pungent and relevant difficulty. The despatch workers, were, to a man, besotted with the problem of *blame.*

Life was materially easier in despatch than it had been on the plant; the despatch area was light, cool, spacious and operatives worked individually, at their own pace at light tasks – quite a contrast to the heat of the ovens, and the heavy, repetitive, and almost unendurably monotonous work on the plant; or the low pay, early mornings, and cantankerous customers that made up the salesman's world. On the other hand the double-edged spiritual weapon of blue-collar 'responsibility' hung heavily over the heads of the despatch men. Whilst they were responsible for ensuring that the work was completed successfully, they were denied the full control which would have made this task relatively light. When this difficulty is connected to a type of work where errors are both particularly likely and especially consequential (as it was in the Wellbread despatch department) then an especially tense form of work culture develops. Basil put it in a nutshell: 'You're always sort of conscious that you can make a mistake, anybody could make a mistake, I've found mistakes that Keith and Donald have made, Keith and I have found mistakes that

Donald has made, and they have found mistakes that I have made
. . . I don't think you could ever avoid making mistakes in that
place'. For Donald, a chargehand, things were worse:

> You'll always make mistakes, whichever way you do it . . . you
> can't be off them (but) they're right to blame you for mistakes,
> because you shouldn't make mistakes . . . it's been a bit of a
> worry lately . . . I lay in bed there, and I try to get to sleep, but
> it's all going through my head . . . I *have* got up at dinner time,
> and my head's been thumping, from worry.

Despatch work was particularly mistake-prone. Work-life consisted of breaking down long production runs of bread into
individual salesman's orders. Fifty or so salesmen's racks (each
with a clip-board and order-sheet attached to it) stood in lines in
the despatch area, and operatives wheeled racks of bread down
these lines, filling, and then ticking off, each completed order. The
necessarily endless repetition of this task often proved fateful, and
a complete rhetoric of jovial guying developed to keep operatives
on their mental, as well as on their physical toes.

Despatch work was a routine made up of minor emergencies.
To quote Hughes (1951, pp. 89, 90):

> The more times per day a man does a given operation, the
> greater his chance of doing it wrong sometimes. . . . And since
> the theoretical probability of making an error some day is
> increased by the very frequency of the operations by which one
> makes one's living, it becomes natural to build up some
> rationale to carry one through. It is also to be expected that
> those who are subject to the same work risks will compose a
> collective rationale which they whistle to one another to keep
> up their courage.

On one occasion this essentially protective cultural structure
broke down. The usual blanket acceptance of mistakes as involuntary was suspended, and two despatch men were sacked for
'dealing'.[3] It is this dramatic and short-lived occasion (mentioned
briefly in a previous volume on the same bakery – Ditton 1977,
pp. 7–8), that I wish to discuss in this, the more obvious ethnographic chapter of this book. However, although the sacking was a
brief incident, its social and structural ramifications were lengthy.

For the two men directly concerned it was very specifically the end of their relationship with Wellbread's. For those more tangentially involved, the little flurry of enforcement activity became a benchmark used at the time, and in later reminiscence, as a resource for rumour, gossip and banter in locker-room exchange. For the analyst, the incident represented the close of a distinct era of despatch history, the culmination of a complete control-wave cycle – one which had begun, some years previously, in the identical circumstances of the sacking of a despatch chargehand for a similar reason.

(ii) EVENT CHRONOLOGY: TREBLE DISASTER

The sacking was a 'disaster'. The sequence of reactions to this disaster correspond closely to the set of responses which typically follow a natural disaster.[4] These have been classified by Powell and Rayner (in Chapman, 1962, pp. 7–23) into seven stages.

1. *Warning:* during which there arises, mistakenly or not, some apprehension based on conditions out of which danger may arise. The affected population often reacts individually, ranging from rigid denial of the threat to exaggerated fear of it. To be effective, the warning must counter ambiguous readings and overcome apathy.

2. *Threat:* during which people are exposed to communications from others, or to signs from the approaching disaster force itself, indicating specific, imminent danger. Often a time when personal estimates concerning the extent of possible loss and the effectiveness of counter-measures are made.

3. *Impact:* during which the disaster strikes, with concomitant death, injury and destruction. The folklore of cataclysm specifies panic at this stage, but it is more likely that those affected respond in a coherent but individual way.

4. *Inventory:* during which those exposed to the disaster begin to form a preliminary picture of what has happened and of their own condition. Again, apparent confusion and aimlessness is quite well organised. Fragmentation may reassert primary groupings, or generate new social groups.

5. *Rescue:* in which activity turns to immediate help for survivors, first aid for the wounded, freeing trapped victims, fighting fires, etc. At this stage, the affected population provides most of its own relief.

6. *Remedy:* during which more deliberate and formal activities are undertaken toward relieving the stricken and their community, both by survivors and by the outside relief agencies that have now moved into the scene.

7. *Recovery:* during which, for an extended period, the community and the individuals in it either recover their former stability or achieve a stable adaptation to the changed conditions which the disaster has brought about.

Cohen (1973) pioneered this kidnapping of natural disaster analysis for the analogical understanding of social upheavals and 'moral panics', and has documented the more basic discrepancies between natural and social disasters.[5] But I found considerable difficulty with the detail of a similar application (although the general drift of the analogy was irresistible) to temporarily interrupted life in the Wellbread despatch department. In sum, at Wellbread's, there could be no agreement that this or that occurrence could be seen as that or the other stage, because the disaster population not only had quite different sets of interests but were also, it seemed, facing different 'disasters'.

For the management, theft was the impact, and sacking the two men concerned the beginnings of a rescue attempt. This sacking, of course, was the impact stage for the two men concerned but, alternatively, functioned as a prior warning for the salesmen. So the event in question affected the researched population in different ways and at different times. Crucially, in terms of their separately identifiable interests, rescue work (all of which had the common characteristic of the allocation of blame)[6] took different directions. The management were consumed by the search for the big *Dealer* ('Who is behind it all?'); the despatch staff were looking for the *Shopper* ('Who split on the two men?'), and the salesmen, believing for a time that more was to come, were grimly seeking the *Squealer* who, they alleged, 'spilt the beans to the management'. I shall describe, in this order, the different directions that such rescue work took.

The Search for the 'Dealer'

The *threat* of impending disaster vaguely presented itself to the bakery management at first in September 1972 – about six months before the actual impact. Some casual reports trickled through, and gradually began to sensitise the management to the possibility that uncontrolled dealing was occurring between despatch and sales staff. Later, Keith, a despatch chargehand, claimed:

> In fact I *did* tell them what was going on way back about six months ago. I went to see the management, but they weren't interested. I told them exactly what was happening, and they just wanted to know the names, and I said: 'If you want to know that much, go in there and find out yourself'. I thought I had to tell them it's going on as it's my job, but I wouldn't tell them the names, and they did nothing about it . . . nothing.

Geoff, an operative on the other shift, recalled why the management did nothing when Keith had previously 'blown the whistle':

> I was on days one particular week, and he said, not to me in particular, but generally, he said: 'There's something funny going on there, I'm going to see into it' . . . you know what Keith is, his attitude, that was before Eadley's time, and he said to both the production manager and the departmental manager, when he saw them after dinner, he said: 'There is a lot of cake going out of here dinner time, and I think there's something funny going on' and he was asked what he meant, and he said: 'There's cake going from A to B in quite large volumes, and I've noticed it before, and perhaps it could account for some of the big losses you're having' . . . and their reply was: 'You be careful what you say, you mustn't say things like that about people, because you could find yourself in serious trouble with them sort of accusations', and it was left at that.[7]

Threat also percolated through to the management from another, internal source. Mr Morrisey, who had been appointed quite recently as a Night Manager ('when I first came here, I was supposed to be the new broom . . . to sort things out'), was immediately convinced that dealing was afoot, although his attempts to procure the evidence had met with repeated failure. He told me, 'I spent two nights sitting up on top of the cake store, I knew stuff was going, I knew who was taking it, I knew the times and everything, but . . . no action'. He persisted, but with the same result. 'I made out a list of everything that was going on, the dates, times, who was involved, and plans for reorganising the whole of the place . . . nothing was done about it'. From the management's point of view, although vague 'fingering' of this sort made the situation look increasingly threatening, nothing apart from heavy suspicion actually accumulated.

Threat became *warning* as the management (now alerted to the possibility of widespread theft by their own employees)[8] became increasingly troubled with the specific (although not yet actionable) hard empirical data of a rising inventory shrinkage rate. This concern even affected the chargehands. Keith recalled:

> Eadly was worried then, we was coming a hell of a lot of bread short then, Donald and all . . . I wasn't involved, so I couldn't cover nothing . . . I was just as worried as anybody, I used to worry myself sick, I used to go round at night counting, I've even gone round at 6 a.m. on a Thursday, and you know how much bread is hanging about then, and I've counted every single loaf we've got to come, added them up on the sheets, work out what's to come in from Broomwich, worked out what's in the bakery, what's coming through the plant, and I've tied the figures down to a dead number, and I've said to myself: 'Right, we're going to be alright in the morning' . . . bloody morning . . . 280 short!

Although now considerably attuned to the possibility that massive dealing was going on, the management did nothing until, by chance, they were presented with actionable evidence (in the form of a signed statement by a witness) of employee 'theft', namely, that on 18 December 1972 Keith, the despatch chargehand, and Doug, an operative on Keith's shift, had illegally taken £76 worth of biscuits from the biscuit store.[9] Keith, ignoring the *impact* that this had on the management, calmly described the occasion as: 'well, a couple of blokes, employed by the firm, see, asked us if we could get them some biscuits, and we said O.K. . . . the money's always useful isn't it?'

Naturally it was possible that this single accusation had wider implications. The impact immediately launched the management into examining a social, as well as a technical *inventory*. The provision of such clearly actionable evidence forced them to indulge in an uncommon form of stocktaking. Crucially, in order to assess the extent of the disaster, they had to quickly discover whether the instance of theft which had been uncovered was UNIQUE (i.e., isolated, and the only one of its kind), or ORDI-

NAL (i.e., one in a series, and thus indicative of other, similar acts). Accordingly, the organising query of the inventory phase, the question, 'How widespread is it?', is in fact in two parts. It firstly demands of the theft size, 'How much of it is going on?' (i.e., how quan*t*itatively widespread), and secondly, of its organisational structure, 'Who is behind it?', in other words, how qua*l*itatively widespread is it? As Fig. 3.1 shows, four different answers are possible.

		THEFT SIZE	
		Large	Small
	Hierarchically organised (corruptor and corruptee)	'Ring'	'Rotten apple
ORGANISATIONAL STRUCTURE (dealer and dealee)[11]	Democratically organised (buyer and seller)	['Tip of] iceberg'	'Pilferage'[10]

FIG. 3.1 *The controllers' inventory*

These four stereotypes of criminal organisation in the factory function as theft control fantasies, occasionally perused and selectively aired to give meaning to emergent events. On this occasion the Wellbread's management decided to interpret the event as one selected from and representative of a series of similar acts, and that consequently the biscuit theft was ordinal and indicative rather than being an unique and isolated act. In addition to this, they selected the 'ring' fantasy as a 'theory' with which they might initially and critically examine the situation. At this stage they professed to believe that a hitherto unnamed employee was the corruptor (or ringleader), with the unfortunate Keith and Doug as corruptee ring-followers. This decision was informed by a procedural dilemma facing the management. The 'ring' fantasy is particularly attractive[12] and, as a working fantasy, it is logical to assume that the 'leader' is not yet revealed. Although Keith and Doug were possible (but weak) candidates for the ringleader stakes, neither immediately demanded unambiguous labelling as the main protagonist. In fact, on close scrutiny, both men revealed curiously ambiguous organisational biographies.

Keith had had a long and hitherto unblemished career at Wellbread's. He was the protégé both of Wally (the Despatch Manager) and Mr Eadley the Bakery Manager. Eadly, in particular, was very upset by the revelations. Keith told me 'Eadley said to me, when he saw me: "I don't know what happened, Keith, but I'll get the rest of the bastards".... I'll always remember that, because he never did anything about it!' Wally also took it badly. Keith again: 'Wally said, he patted me on the shoulder and said: "Oh, Keith, I wouldn't have believed it of you, anybody else, yes, but you, Oh, no, Keith ... you're the last person I would have suspected", he kept patting his heart'. To counterbalance this, it was remembered that it was Keith who had, six months earlier, 'shopped' others in a vague and general way. In the light of the recent exposure this was now seen as being particularly base (although as a matter of fact, it was almost entirely the management's failure to act on that occasion which had pushed Keith to subsequently take up dealing).[13] Accordingly, Keith was, in Klapp's (1956, p. 338) terms, typed as an 'invisible deceiver'.

Doug similarly presented an ambivalent work character, although in a different way. Although Doug had no personal record of dishonesty, he was tarred with the Philips brush. His brother, Dan Philips, once a chargehand at Wellbread's, had been sacked for dealing in 1970, three years before (see note 8, at end). By an ironic twist as potent as that which transformed Keith into a dealer (see note 13) Dough always felt that he had been spuriously given a bad name for which he might as well be hung. He told me:

> Then Dan got the sack, and by rights, it [the job of chargehand] should have been mine, really, as Keith will tell you. Eadley promised it to me, he said: 'On my word, the job will be yours', so when Dan got the sack, Eadley called me into the office and said: 'I've put your name forward for the chargehand's job', but Mr Smarteagh didn't agree, ... I thought the reason for that was that Dan was my brother, and he got sacked for fiddling. That's how I saw it, because they never had no other reason to say I couldn't do it, I always done it right when I done it [i.e. as a holiday relief].

Of course, when Doug was caught revenging his imputed deviance; Smarteagh was seen to have originally made a wise decision. In Klapp's (1956, p. 338) terms, Doug was a 'visible rogue'. As Wally, the Despatch Manager put it (according to Keith): 'Other funny thing was that Wally nearly had a heart attack, he kept patting his heart, and he said "I'm not surprised about you at all, Douglas, you look a rogue", that didn't please Doug at all I'm afraid, "Fucking cheek", he said . . . he thinks they've always had it in for him since his brother was sacked'.

Having adopted the 'ring' fantasy, the management swiftly moved to the *rescue* phase of the disaster by consecutively interviewing Keith and Doug, extracting a written acknowledgement of guilt from each, and sacking the pair of them. In order to describe features of the control-wave which dramatically followed this reaction, we need both a vocabulary and a format for using it to comparatively analyse the 'Informants' – the key figures in the control-wave.

The basic resource of the informer is 'talk'. But talk, itself, comes in various FORMS. An informer may, firstly, 'confess' (wherein he would 'talk' about himself only), or declare 'the acknowledgement of fault or offence to others through the formal declaration of injury' (Hepworth and Turner, 1974, p. 32). Sometimes 'confessing' is strategic and is done merely to gain the respect, and thus, it is hoped, the mercy of the accuser, because it is believed that the accuser already has sufficient evidence to sustain a successful prosecution, but would like a 'confession' to bureaucratically ease the work of prosecution. Secondly, a particularly dastardly informer may 'shop', and 'talk' about the misdeeds of others only. The informer's self (with guilty knowledge) may often be protected by claiming that knowledge has only just become sufficient to warrant exposure (if 'shop' was voluntary), or that one's knowledge is incomplete (if 'shop' was forced). Thirdly, a wholly unrestrained informant may 'squeal', or talk unreservedly about both his personal misdeeds and those of others. Again, like 'shopping', this may be done to cravenly gain immunity for the self (as did Valachi)[14] or because the informer believes that he has already been 'shopped' by another. A fourth logically possible resource (not, alas, available to informers) is to keep 'mum', and refuse to 'talk' at all.

The RANGE of talk is as important as its form. 'Talk' may be either *specific* (where the range of talk is narrow, and restricted to token or example offences); *limited* (where the range of talk is strategic. Here, the informer details an impressive selection of several offences of a relevant nature from the total he is informed about); or, finally, *unlimited* (where the talk range is broad, and the informer details all those offences known to him).

Another crucial dimension is the TIMING of talk. Naturally, 'talk' may be *backdated* (and thus about offences which have occurred outside the scope of organisational recall, or, more formally, those which are excluded by statutes of limitation), *current* (offences falling within the scope of organisational recall, and which may thus be recoverable for prosecution purposes) or *postdated* ('talk' about offences soon to take place, whose in-stigators may subsequently be caught *in flagrante delicto*).

In these terms, both Keith and Doug 'confessed' to a specific, current offence as dealers. But this format is incomplete. Keith and Doug were both sacked 'instatate', that is, no character was definitely allocated to them (whilst, in role terms, they were inevitably dealers there were no grounds for saying which party had instigated the deal), and the total size of the theft series in question was unclear. However, the bakery management pro-ceeded with a second line of rescue work – 'putting the frighteners on'. Selected members of the total workforce (despatch staff and wholesale salesmen) were interviewed as a step toward trying to winkle out 'Mr Big' or 'The Godfather'[15] – the working title now given to the still as yet unnamed arch-corruptor.

On 20 and 21 February (Keith and Doug had been sacked at 11 a.m. on the 20th) Mr Eadley and Mr Smarteagh consecutively and individually interviewed all the despatch staff. The manager-ial line was that Keith had 'squealed', and that accordingly it was in each man's best interests to simply tell all he knew. Doug told me:

What actually happens is that they get someone in the office, and they say: 'Well, look here, lad, you might as well tell us everything what's been going on, because your mate has al-ready told us, so why don't you admit it, and tell us the rest of it?' hoping that the bloke will say: 'Well, if my mate has told, I might as well do likewise' . . . that's what they tried with me, but I didn't say nothing.

Doug added: 'I don't know whether they had any information,

you can't really say, they may have just been guessing and trying to get a little bit more'. Although this would have been fairly obvious in retrospect, the rhetoric of confrontation meant that 'talk' was likely and that, further, the type of line adopted was sufficiently ambiguously phrased to allow a weak informant to adopt any of the three talking *forms*. However, for various reasons (chiefly that the interviewees were forewarned about the content of the interview, and thus the element of surprise was missing), the interviewing was not very effective. But the pressure *did* lead one man to crack. Basil (an operative on Keith's shift) became an informant by 'confessing' to a limited range of backdated offences as a corruptee dealer of small amounts. The crucial implication of this confession was that it necessarily implied that (if Basil was a corruptee) 'Mr Big' was a salesman.

At 3 p.m. on the next day (22 February) the bakery management interviewed all the wholesale salesmen. Again the management claimed to 'know everything', and were merely bent upon tidying up some details before announcing the identity of 'Mr Big'. Keith told me:

> Eadley said he would name Mr Big on Thursday [the next day] although who Mr Big was, I don't know . . . he said that he would denounce Mr Big on the Thursday! . . . yes (laugh) Oh, yes! it was all done . . . he said that there was a big man involved, he was on Sales, the governor on Sales, the man who negotiated all the terms and had been getting them the cakes . . . and all that.

But again this was not massively effective, although it had the desired effect upon two wholesalers who cracked and became informants, offering 'confessions' to a limited range of backdated offences as corruptee dealers in inconsequential amounts. The implication, exasperatingly, was that the elusive 'Mr Big' was suddenly reborn as a despatch man. Although the rescue phase had produced three additional illicit participants (Basil, and Bert and Claude the two salesmen), all three had 'confessed' to small, backdated, limited-range offences as corrupt*ees*. Whilst this logically assumes the presence of a corrupt*or*, rescue work had produced no authentic candidate to fit the controller's 'ring' fantasy as a ring*leader*.

Obviously, this posed a problem. The initial (albeit contingent) managerial allegiance to the 'ring' fantasy could not be sustained in the light of long-term lack of sympathetic evidence. On the other hand the three additional confessions indicated the presence of a corruptor. What was the *remedy*? At this stage, the Wellbread's management reviewed its control-fantasy alternatives. Both of the democratic alternatives ('tip of the iceberg', or 'pilferage') were ruled out by the confessions which had indicated a hierarchical organisational structure. The failure to identify a 'Mr Big' spoilt the 'ring' fantasy. By exclusion (of alternatives) and by deduction (from corruptee claims) this only left the management with the 'rotten apple' fantasy.

At this precise juncture the management struck an astute bargain between the 'facts' and the fantasies by making two compromises. Firstly, the size of the theft series under consideration was reduced to small (in line with information collected by confession), and secondly, the organisational characters of Keith and Doug (who were sacked 'instatate' on this issue) were promoted to corrupt*or*. In the eyes of many, Keith and Doug now *became* respectively 'Mr Big' and 'The Godfather'. This settlement concluded the period of remedy, and enabled the management to move into a period of equilibrium-restoring *recovery*.

Recovery implies resurrection of a replica social system to that which existed before the impact. For the Wellbread's management this did not mean that they had now to prevent all thefts but that, whilst saving some 'face', shrinkage should be (unknowingly) allowed to resume its normal functional levels. Face-work included the temporary enforcement of the rule that the salesmen should not 'hold' bread on their vans overnight, and the eventual departure of Basil, thus leaving a clean despatch team. As for loss-work, although dealing was temporarily suspended during managerial investigations, as control pressure eased, dealing recovered under the constant pressure for uniformity of illicit supply felt by salesmen. In plain language, restoring equilibrium meant restoring dealing. As Geoff put it:

I think they deserve to lose everything they lost . . . because, going back to the same thing again, the whole system that is Wellbread's scream out for it, they ask for it . . . it's not a case of sacking everybody on despatch and bringing in new people to run despatch . . . that's not the answer to it . . . that's only part of the answer . . . the whole system which they work in just sit up and beg for pilfering, and for these sort of things to build up, they all build up from small things, and unless there's a strict rein held on it by either the foreman in despatch, or else the manager who works in despatch, that'll happen again because the system ask for it.

In fact, how *did* the despatch staff feel about the search for 'Mr Big' and 'The Godfather'? How did the management's disaster affect the workforce?

The Search for the 'Shopper'

The curious thing about 'social' as opposed to natural disasters is not just that they have a different effect upon different people, nor that they are distinguished by a simple class effect (fires, floods and so on may affect working-class areas more severely than better positioned and superior middle-class ones), but crucially, in social disasters, events have a qualitatively different *meaning* for different classes of victims. At Wellbread's for example, what seemed to the management to be part of rescue-work following the impact of a report of theft (i.e., the sacking of Keith and Doug) struck Keith and Doug, literally, as the unannounced impact of their own personal disaster.

Thus the *impact* hit the despatch staff, totally without threat or warning, at 11 a.m. on 20 February 1973 (see Fig. 3.2, opposite). As Keith recalled:

First thing I heard was when Eadley came and told me that Smarteagh wanted to see me in the office, well, you see I immediately thought it was something to do with the Union . . . so I went in there, and there were these two security men from H.Q. in there with him, well, he told them they could wait outside, and there was just him, and Eadley in the corner, scribbling notes. Smarteagh said to me: 'I've got a signed statement here alleging that you and the said Douglas Philips took £76 worth of biscuits on December 18th, do you plead Guilty or Not Guilty?'

Surprise was effective. Keith told me later: 'Well, they wouldn't have got us if we'd had the time . . . if Eadley had said to me in the morning, 'Mr Smarteagh wants to see you later about some biscuits that were taken before Christmas', then I would have gone to see Doug, and we would have imagined up some fantastic story to cover ourselves'. However, as Keith admitted much later:

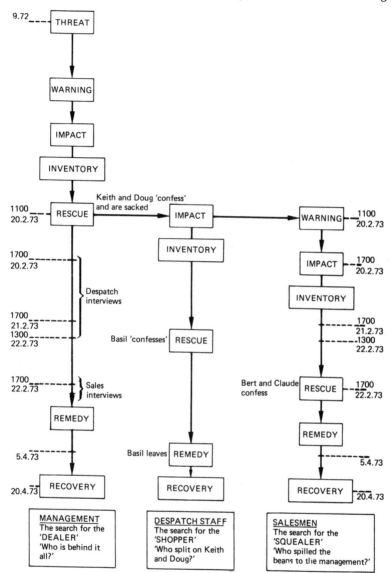

FIG. 3.2 *A treble disaster*

It is very difficult when you're confronted with something not to open your mouth . . . you've just got to sit tight, you don't get time to think. . . . I was confronted, when they had me in the office, but I had the foresight to think first, and all I said was that I wanted a solicitor . . . and that sort of threw them off their guard for a minute, which allowed me to gather my senses . . . but had he started bawling and shouting as I've no doubt that he *would* do, Smarteagh, then I may well have said more than I wanted to say, but I just said that I wanted a solicitor, and momentarily, that threw him off his guard . . . because he wasn't expecting me to say anything like that.

Although immediately denying the accusation ('Well, the first thing I said was "What a load of rubbish, let me see that statement"'), Keith soon had second thoughts ('Then I thought for a bit, see, and I thought "Well, if they do that [i.e. go to the police], the amount of stuff that I've nicked in my time, I might get 12 years!"') and said:

> 'Well, I admit to that, except for that bit which includes Doug Philips, I did it by myself'. . . . He then said that I'd have to pay back all the money, and of course, it meant 'instant dismissal', and I said: 'Of course, obviously'.[16]

Doug's experience was similar:

> Keith went in to see Smarteagh, and I didn't even know he had gone in there, he just disappeared, and that's nothing unusual, he often disappears for 20 minutes sometimes . . . I was working on the machine, and Eadley came out and said 'Mr Smarteagh wants to see you', and I had an idea that it was something about bread or something like that, you know. I went into the office and he put the statement in front of me, and give me the choice of whether I wanted to deny it and call the police, or sign it and have my cards . . . I said 'Well, if you know it all, you know it all, I might as well sign and go', and he said 'My advice is that that is the best thing you can do' . . . which I done, and I said 'Is that the finish of it completely?', and he said 'Yes, that's the finish', and Eadley said 'You've got my word on it' . . . so I signed, and he said 'What about overloading the wholesalers?', and I said 'I'm not going to say anything else', and I went.

The *inventory* period in the disaster faced by despatch staff had two distinct phases: an initial 'divisive' phase and a later 'unifying' phase which paved the way for rescue work. In the early phase, workers took preliminary inventories (i.e., decided 'what was going on') very much in terms of differing personal concerns. At this stage the uncombined response of the workforce suited managerial tactics very well: out of such cleverly conceived and constructed anomie, informant 'talk' most easily emerges.

Relative to the sacking of Keith and Doug, despatch workers fell into three groups (the Guilty, the Suspected and the Innocent) each constructing a different preliminary inventory. The Guilty, Keith and Doug, had guilty knowledge of the incident in question. It is a nice irony that, after extensive investigation, the Wellbread's management perceived and described the situation in terms ('rotten apples') as far removed as possible from the situation described by participants as existing prior to managerial control action. As Donald, the other chargehand, put it, 'Well, to tell you the truth, everybody was having a dabble out of it . . . everybody was having a share, the whole despatch as far as I knew'. On the ground, the dealing pattern closely resembled the 'tip of the iceberg' fantasy. Seven out of the eight currently employed despatch staff were at that time, or had in the past, worked illicitly as dealers, of one sort or another (see Ditton, 1977, Ch. 4). In the light of this, the Guilty shared with the Suspected (the other despatch men with dealer stains on their characters who had, thus, private general guilty knowledge) the concern 'Will the impact spread?' The version worrying the Guilty was 'Will we get blamed for the lot?' Although both Keith and Doug had secured guarantees that their signed confessions were the end of the matter as far as they were concerned, neither felt that this would halt the spread of malicious rumour. Both already knew that they had already agreed to repay more biscuits than they took. Keith said:

> We already have [been over-blamed], we didn't take anything like £76 worth, we only got £15 worth between us. We've had to pay for all the shortages for the whole week, there's the biscuits for Cyril Grimes [storeman], some for his boy to take home, some for the woman who works up there.

Although Doug was relatively stoic and 'philosophical' about it, being a scapegoat rankled with Keith, who was eternally struck with the unfairness of it all:

> What gets you is that it's so unfair, I did it, I know, but there's

20 or 30 blokes up there who are doing something like it, if I wanted to, I could go up there now, and tell them of all the other fiddles. . . . It's unfair really, I've been there for 12 years, one slip-up and I get the sack. . . . I know we'll get scapegoated for everything now, everything that's gone missing for the last two years will be Douglas and me . . . we'll get the blame for everything now.

The Suspected had a slightly different concern. They were all (Donald, Basil, Barney and Geoff) despatch workers who knew what was going on from either current (Donald and Basil) or past (Geoff and Barney) personal experience as dealers. As Keith put it, 'they've all got to go and see Smarteagh, the finger's on everybody'. Geoff remembered what this period was like:

You all know that you take the chances, and if you're caught, you take the consequences of it . . . that's the start and the finish of it to my mind . . . to be honest, it's worried me for months . . . I didn't know exactly how they were doing it, or where they were getting it.

The Suspected's version of the general worry about impact spread was 'Will we get caught?' When Keith came out of Smarteagh's office he bumped into Wally, the Despatch Manager: 'his face was drained of all its colour, not its usual red, you know . . . I should think Basil was fucking worried too, I saw him later, and his face was as white as a sheet, I should think he thought he was next'. Basil told, graphically, what he felt like:

You know what I feel like? I feel like I'm in a battlefield . . . like I'm walking forward with lots of men, and all the others are machine-gunned down, and here I am, still walking, without a scratch.

This sudden sensitivity to blame paralysed many otherwise innocuous work tasks. Geoff refused to go near the roundsmen in the morning ('it gives you a feeling of uncomfortableness'), and Donald wouldn't go to the cake-store without a chaperone; 'if anything goes missing in the next few days, they'll blame me . . . you come with me, I'm not going up there by myself'.

The Innocent, Rob and Larry (and the plant men) saw the whole thing differently. The first reaction was disbelief. One said 'I still can't believe he done it, but I suppose he must have done if he got the sack. . . . I just can't imagine Keith getting *anything* away!' A counter-reaction was a glut of contradictory rumour. I interviewed Jim, a casual worker in despatch, on the night of the sacking. He told me 'The whole bakery's talking about it, and you hear about 16 different stories, and the whole thing gets slightly warped as it goes round'. But the Innocents' lack of experience or knowledge made them easy prey for managerial definitions. Most soon accepted the managerial 'rotten apples' definition, but with an interesting corollary. Keith and Doug were not pilloried for being dealers (or, more subtly, for getting caught) but for being *immoral* dealers. Generally they were seen as having been 'too greedy', or to have gone 'too far'. One man said, 'Keith and Doug would have been alright if they'd stuck to bread, nobody would have said anything . . . their mistake was going into biscuits', and a plant man thought the issue to be even simpler: 'they were daft, really, they boasted about it in here [locker room], they should have kept quiet about it'. Rob thought that they had been 'too obvious', and that it had all got (again, immorally) out of hand:

> Articles out of the bakery used to go missing, and it didn't take anybody to work it out [i.e., who it was], cables, tables, heaters, all sorts of things . . . that's stupid, really.

Keith, in retrospect, not only felt that things had got out of hand, but also that they had got 'too organised'. He told me:

> When I got it organised so that everybody got a fair cut, then actually the total went up from 12 trays a day, and the final total was, I think, 28 trays . . . at holiday time, that was a rack each, some of them were taking; Christmas, all the wholesalers had a rack each . . . 15 racks of bread! . . . we got everything highly organised, we got a price list out for different items although we never had any scale of charges on the cake, see, they just used to give us what they thought, what it was worth.

However within 24 hours both the Guilty (who left) and the Innocent (who drifted back to work) became uninvolved, leaving the Suspected to face the managerial music alone. This, together with the fact that clearer knowledge of the sacking percolated through, meant that the initial diversity of questioning melded into one unified and crucial query. In this collective, final inventory, the question on all the men's lips was 'Who split on Keith and Doug?' The search for the 'Shopper' was on. It was here that a larger search (for 'Mr Big') was getting under way, and managerial interviews with the despatch men began. So knowledge about managerial sources, and the extent and quality of their information was crucial to interviewee success. Again those questioned reacted closely in terms of their personal distance from dealing.

The Innocent were prepared by Mr Morrisey the night manager: 'If you've got a clear conscience over all this, don't worry, if anybody actually accuses you of this, just tell them to tell it to your solicitor, and do them for defamation of character'. However, interviews with the Innocent were perfunctory and nothing was revealed. Later one Innocent, Rob Siddell, was able to retrospectively reinterpret some hitherto inexplicable events. He told me:

> It was going on from the first day, I mean many a time there's been a rack of bread, a full rack on stock, and I've been out playing darts, and I've come back, and there's only been five or six trays left . . . and I've seen Keith give Doug pound notes, and Doug stick them in his pocket.

Of the Suspected, those with backdated dealer connections got off lightly, with both Barney and Geoff being offered Keith's job as chargehand before Geoff finally accepted it. Those with current dealer connections, the weak link in the despatch defence, were a different matter. Wally didn't deal with the salesmen, but he had been pilfering his petty cash and fiddling the stock-sheets and the cash-sale sheets to cover it for years. Donald was a big dealer in his own right. An ex-salesman (moved into the bakery to pay off a large amount that he had 'delayed paying' back to the firm, see Ditton, 1977, p. 141), he had been promoted over Doug when Doug's brother, Dan Philips, had been sacked for dealing. Keith claimed of Donald:

> I would say that Donald was making nigh on £60 per week on nights, plus all his free groceries and everything, well, he could afford to give . . . he used to give Geoff so much of that . . . he used to give the blokes on the plant a fiver *each*! . . . and still be making £40 clear.

Basil, on Keith's shift, was a major influence on the expansion of Keith's and Doug's dealing, and an equal participant with them in most of the deals that took place on that shift. Basil was the collector: he used to tour the salesmen's loading bays on Saturday mornings with a list of bread dealt during the week and collect money owed. For this, he was unaffectionately known by the wholesalers as 'Rachman'. As well as this, although Keith ran all dealing (by covering all losses), Basil was the 'brain' behind many organisational improvements. For example, although Keith was initially against it ('I wouldn't wear it, I didn't think it was fair'), he finally gave in to Basil and agreed that the traditional price of 25p a tray should be increased to 50p. Keith remembered the occasion particularly well:

> Basil said that he wasn't going to risk his job for 5/– a tray, so they decided to put the price up, but they [wholesalers] refused it, they said they weren't going to pay 10/– . . . this went on for two days, and then they came crawling . . . the wholesalers held a meeting with Doug and Basil, in the despatch, they agreed on that, and from then on it was 10/–.

At the same time, rolls (which had been free to dealees) were charged for. This move was fatal. Henceforth the salesmen would commercially, but not socially, support the dealer network. For a while the balance of trade was upset as Donald was still supplying on the day shift at the old price, although eventually he and Keith agreed not to cut each other's business. This cartel persisted until Keith was sacked.

On top of all this Basil was also dealing on the side for extra. When Keith discovered this, he furiously closed all dealing down. As he recalls 'We stopped it for a bit, and then things started to slip again . . . Basil came up to me one morning, crying on my shoulders "I can't manage on the money, Keith" . . . and so forth, so it all started again'. Heavy irony descended upon events again at this point (see note 13, at end). Firstly, before Keith was involved in dealing (when he was suspicious that it was going on) he tried to blame Broomwich (the other production bakery in the Wellbread's chain) for the losses, and this was later read as a spurious attempt to deflect blame from himself. Secondly, he had voiced suspicions about Basil. After the sacking this was also seen as quite dastardly. Basil takes up the story:

Apparently over the last few months Keith's been pointing the finger at me, that's what Wally was telling me anyway, apparently, whenever he's been short on his stock, he's been saying to Wally 'Watch Basil' . . . well, that'll count towards me now, won't it? He's been trying to make me look suspicious, and that'll make him look bad now.

Thirdly, with amazing coincidence, Basil was not with Keith and Doug on the night of the biscuit theft, as a punishment for dealing on the side! Keith sadly recalled:

Doug and me discovered that Basil was trying to con us, because he was dealing with other people besides us . . . of course, Doug put the idea into my head, 'Why didn't we make an extra shilling?' and that's how we became involved.

However, when the impact struck, both Basil and Donald knew that they would be lucky to survive. The slight warning they had, on the other hand, proved invaluable. Basil and Donald got together and prepared an identical, self-protective line, 'you know, Donald said, "you scratch my back, and I'll scratch yours"', and Donald also got together with Wally. Donald recalled, 'we were working it out, you see, what to tell them . . . I said "We'll show them this 70 spare as the men's bread", and he said "No, tell them it's 42"!' Although Wally was not interviewed (as far as the men knew), Donald claimed to have battled it out and kept 'mum'. He reported publicly 'Smarteagh said "How much did I know?", but I don't know anything about it, and anyway it's not my principle to say anything like that, I do my job and that's that'. Later, in private, he claimed to me that 'Basil's asked me to put the bubble on all the others'; but that he abstained.

Basil was a different matter. His first interview went fairly well. He remembered:

I got the third degree yesterday. Eadley and Wally had me in their office, and they kept firing questions at me, one stood behind me, and one stood in front. 'Did you put any extra on the wholesalers?' . . . I got wise then, and said: 'Sorry? . . . you've got the advantage of me, I don't know what you're talking about', he just patted me on the shoulder and said that they hadn't finished with me yet, and that Smarteagh would want to see me today.

In the second interview, he was told that Keith 'shopped' him. 'He [Eadley] said that they knew I was involved as well, he said that Keith had told them everything he knew, he said that they hadn't asked him to, he had just volunteered the information, so I said that I *had* been involved, but that I wasn't any more . . . I used to have a few cakes and things, but it got out of hand, and I didn't have any more to do with it'.

Basil's 'confession', although too limited and backdated to be of much value to the management, proved to be the turning point in the impact on despatch. By claiming corrupt*ee* status, Basil had inexorably transferred the search for 'Mr Big' to the salesmen. The pressure thus off despatch, it now became possible to rationally and coolly assess the various theories which had been circulating about 'who split on Keith and Doug?' and begin *rescue* work.

The official answer was that nobody had 'split', but that two security men from H.Q. on a routine nightly check (H.Q. was 90 miles away: no such checks had been announced before) had seen and reported the theft. This line all too easily fits the myth of conventional enforcement activity (with the goodies catching the baddies red-handed), and was immediately doubted by those closely or intimately involved. As Geoff put it 'that didn't just ring right to me, I just couldn't accept [that that was] the way it happened'. Keith could see that the story was internally inconsistent, and so proposed an alternative:

Well, they said that the H.Q. security men discovered it, but they weren't there, they knew so much detail, if they'd known about it all that time, they wouldn't have waited until now to sack us . . . they wouldn't have let us work here, on nights by ourselves, until now, would they? No . . . somebody shopped us I reckon, they knew too much detail . . . I expect H.Q. came down here and looked at the figures, and said: 'You must do something about this', and they must have got the fifth bloke for something else, and he shopped us.

Although Doug was a little chary of naming names ('I wouldn't accuse anyone until I was one hundred per cent certain, which I don't think any one really is, although it points that way, you can't accuse people until you really know'.), Keith's preliminary search for a likely character for the 'shopper' produced Alfred, an employee at the garage, from whom they had borrowed a torch on the night in question. The torch was needed for the break-in, and the biscuit store is located near enough to the garage for Alfred to see the whole operation. Keith was convinced. Alfred had been involved (albeit marginally) in the heist, but not in the repercussions. Also events which had occurred, but which Alfred did not know about ('they didn't mention anything about the ladder, or the fact that we broke the window') were never brought up formally. Some doubt remained, however, as to exactly why he had 'talked'. Keith initially suspected some simple managerial pressure, with subsequent 'shopping' exchanged for punishment. Geoff suggested the probable scenario to me:[17]

> They probably scared him a little by taking him to the office and saying 'Look, we know this has happened, what have you got to say?' . . . like a sort of police technique of interrogation . . . I suspect that's what's happened, by getting statements from one or two persons, and having others in the office and more or less bluffing them, because I can't see that they had concrete evidence against them.

Keith suggested that Alfred was probably blackmailed. 'I expect they got this chap up at the garage for filling up his car or something, and they were about to sack him, and he said "What about all the others?" . . . and they said "Tell us everything" . . . and he did'. A more sophisticated version (but with a similar cast of characters) later emerged. It gradually came to be believed that the most likely course of events was that Billy Grimes (the garage foreman, and the son of Cyril Grimes the storeman) had overheard Alfred gossiping about Keith and Doug's exploits, and subsequently persuaded him to report the event formally because Billy was worried that the health of his father, Cyril, would deteriorate further if the unexplained losses at the biscuit store were not pinned on somebody. Geoff offered a particularly benign version of this tale:

> That [losses] was making him [Cyril] . . . he was getting towards a breakdown, that was really upsetting his home-life and everything, he was losing say £100–200 worth of stuff per week, and apparently he was the only one with a key . . . I think suspicion must have been pointed at him, . . . his son, was also foreman in the garage . . . and that happened to come to his

son's ears, now, what's a son going to do when his father's being
made ill? . . . I think that Billy probably saw them up there one
night [or] . . . things that happen up there probably circulated
around the men that work in the garage, and that came to his
son's ears.

For a while this 'shopper' theory vied with other speculative
and imaginative proposals suggested by the uninvolved. One
plant man suggested 'I've got my own personal theory about who
did it, and that was Mr Morrisey . . . he never did get on with
Keith, they've hated each other's guts ever since Morrisey came
here', and Larry, one of the (few) innocent despatch men, suggested an alternative, ingenious family connection. 'Keith
threatened to poke Fatty [Siddell, the head cleaner] didn't he?
Perhaps his son [Rob Siddell] told him something what was going
on . . . they're father and son, aren't they? . . . perhaps he was
worried that his son would get involved if he didn't say anything'.
Now, although both Fatty and Rob are conspicuously honest
(both sometimes even paying for the bread that they take home
each day), and Rob was on holiday during the sacking ('I was in
London, my Dad rang me . . . he asked me "Did you have
anything to do with it?" and I said "No" . . . and he said "Thank
Christ for that"'), it is unlikely that Fatty would have said
anything without *first* discovering whether or not Rob was involved, or that either of them would have had sufficient evidence
to indict Keith and Doug. Thus, the theory of Alfred-the-
'shopper' was never seriously challenged.

But nothing was ever *done* about Alfred. No campaign energy
was wasted on retribution. It was enough to just *know* that Alfred
was the mysterious 'shopper' and, however barbarous and dis-
ruptive his behaviour might be, at least his information was
limited to one event.

A residual problem for management was the ambiguous position of Basil. Whilst he had admitted to offences, they lay outside
the actionable scope (or organisational recall) of control at
Wellbread's. He was an enigma. A self-confessed, but still employed 'thief'. Ironically, whilst Basil's confession rescued despatch, his continued employment posed awkward problems for
both management and men. Geoff put it in a nutshell:

Eadley also told me that Basil had been honest enough to tell him that he was in on this as well, you see . . . but then, how do you account for him still to be there? still be in his job? That's where it fall down, you see. . . . Unless he turned Queen's evidence, how's he there?

However, with his dealer network suspended, and because he was now seen as sufficiently untrustworthy to be allowed into other deals, Basil got dissatisfied. He had also been transferred to Donald's shift, where he did not fit in well. Apparently 'Donald caught Basil laying off some more bread to the wholesalers, there was a heated exchange of words, from what I can gather, and Basil said he was going to leave'. Eventually Basil solved the problem by voluntarily leaving Wellbread's (and going, with Keith and Doug, to Trotters, the meat-pie factory) on 5 April, just over six weeks after Keith and Doug were sacked.

As soon as this *remedy* was digested, *recovery* was almost immediate. Considerable pressure was facing the despatch dealers (Donald, and now Geoff) to resume dealing. Every morning stock bread (which would normally have illicitly flowed to the salesmen) piled up rackful upon embarrassing rackful. One morning when I worked (3.3.73), instead of the usual 30 loaves or so, we had 402 loaves left over! Donald said: 'Look at all this bloody stock! . . . fucking stuff's everywhere, I don't know what to do with it all!' This matched the salesmen's problem of an unchanged illicit demand, and a suddenly suspended illicit supply. Both dealers and dealees also had h.p. payments to keep up, and families to support. Keith sadly and prophetically told me 'well, I think, I'll give them a month and they'll start up again'. He over-estimated. Dealing was in full swing again within three weeks. Recovery was rapid, and complete.

The Search for the 'Squealer'

The sacking of Keith and Doug (which initiated the rescue of managerial problems, and generated the impact of the despatch men's disaster) provided a nice *warning* to salesmen that, at least, dealing would have to be suspended for a while.

Luckily the sacking occurred at 11 a.m. – an almost perfect time if salesmen are to be allowed to conceal their dealing. At this time in the morning little bread had been put out on the salesmen's racks for the next day's trade, and there was no 'hot' bread about. Had the sacking occurred at 3 a.m., then most of the salesmen's racks would have been bulging with suddenly conspicuous 'extra' bread, and many would have been caught red-handed. It is not that the management cannot be bothered to get out of bed to catch factory miscreants. In 1968, in the middle of the winter, Eadley and two other managers hid in the hedge surrounding the bakery, and at about 3.30 a.m., stopped and searched the wholesale van driven by Lonny, one of the longest serving salesmen. Keith filled in the background for me:

> See, '—' (a previous biscuit storekeeper) was losing stuff galore, but he wasn't saying nothing about it, because he was doing it himself, he knew he was losing more stuff, but he daren't say anything because they may have started investigating all round, so he kept his mouth shut . . . he was only putting down the stock of about £15–£20 a week, short, but in actual fact they was losing about £600 a week worth of stuff . . . yeah, well, you know how much stuff they took off Lonny's van that morning . . . £240 worth!

Doug saw this early event as, as he put it, 'the beginning of the biscuits'. In terms of blame, the occasion *did* share some features with his own demise. He recalled:

> '—' (previous biscuit storekeeper) was going into the office, see, and saying 'Well, that's the night shift', you see, 'the night shift keep taking these biscuits' . . . well then . . . the volume increased, and eventually Lonny got caught see, and then they put the blame down to Lonny, but he only actually got done for that week, [but] he had to pay back £350, that's how the biscuits started.

Not only was Lonny not sacked, he was suspended on full pay for a short while, and then completely reinstated on to his old round (and all his old fiddles). This combination of leniency and outright cheek even staggered George, an experienced and important dealee-salesman. He commented (see Ditton, 1977, p. 109 *et passim*): 'Christ Almighty! . . . he'd only been back two weeks, and he came up to me and said "Could I get him into the cheap bread" . . . just like that'. Such seemingly capricious enforcement policy is, in fact, extremely systematic. It is not just that the management sympathise with the salesmen, but that they point-blank *refuse* to criminalise instances of salesman irregularity. As Geoff put it 'Smarteagh's been a salesman himself, he knows what goes on, he must do . . . there's a certain amount they're prepared to close their eyes to'. To be blunt, the management close both eyes to fiddling (where customers lose) and one eye to dealing and pilfering. The one eye that remains open in the latter case is firmly transfixed upon the inside men. This is a publicly and widely acknowledged sentiment known as 'Smarteagh's Rule'. Keith explained it to me:

> Well, Smarteagh's always said, he's got a special thing about the men who work inside, the suppliers, without them there would be no trouble, the suppliers are the blokes who start it, and the receivers should be pitied.

As Keith put it, if they really wanted to stop dealing, then (after Mailer), you hit the one irrefutable factor in the whole deal pyramid: the user. Keith suggested that they 'should have Morrisey doing spot checks on the vans, after they'd loaded, before they loaded . . . all the returns which come back should be checked by a person like Wally, and when I say checked, I mean checked thoroughly every day . . . rigid control, that's the only thing that'll stop it'. But the Wellbread management have traditionally ignored deleterious information about salesmen dealing because, Keith continued:

> They didn't *want* to know, they just didn't want to know . . . and they *still* don't want to know about this bread, because if they wanted to know about it, and really and truly wanted to know about it, they would have had this lot out, and they still haven't had it out . . . they want it to stop, but they don't want to do anything about it.

It was equally clear (from the timing of the sacking) that in the current control wave the Wellbread's management was not interested in tracing salesman dealees. Periodically knocking holes in the fabric of the sales team, which are just filled by replacement salesmen (and new potential dealees), is, in the absence of any systemic changes, quite pointless. No, at this stage (20 February) the management chose to turn their usual commercially blinded enforcement eye on corruptee dealee salesmen, merely using them, it was hoped, to reveal the name of 'Mr Big', who they still assumed (and continued to do so until Basil's 'confession' on the 22nd) was, in accordance with Smarteagh's Rule, an inside man.

But although this nice warning meant that the salesmen could prepare for the imminent impact, it did not mean that they could avoid it. In preparation, the salesmen knew that they could no longer depress legitimate bread orders so as to accommodate illicit supply. This provided something of a dilemma. To suddenly *increase* bread orders at a time like this is unavoidably to display that one was previously dealing. *Not* to increase bread orders to make up the illicit shortfall is to fail to satisfy those customers who have unwittingly been accepting illicit supply, and to chance their reporting this doubly indicative failure to the Wellbread's management. It is at times like these that some basic conflicts shine through the usual mutual interest which binds unscrupulous salesmen and despatch staff (see Ditton, 1977, p. 113 *et passim*), giving the salesmen the problem of equalising the potential visibility of deals with the continuity of sales.

The impact struck the salesmen at 5 p.m. on 20 February. At this time of day salesmen return to the bakery from their rounds, and adjust their bread orders for the next day to cope with daily demand (and invisible illicit supply) contingencies. As each dealee salesman heard what had happened to Keith and Doug, he knew he had to choose between looking conspicuous at the bakery by ordering extra bread, or letting customers down. On the night of the 20th, and for the next week or so, the salesmen practised one or more of several well-known solutions to the problem of a suddenly dry illicit supply. George, a wholesale salesman with a lot to lose, described how he had increased stealing from the firm to make up the slack:

> I *have* done it . . . I have done it in the past when things have been a bit tight, I've been and got myself a couple of trays of stales. . . . When Keith and the others were caught, it was madness for a few days, I mean, you have to cover what you have been getting don't you? . . . otherwise it would show . . . especially at a time like that, when they're looking for that sort of thing.

Alternatively, salesmen can increase the amounts that they fiddle from customers. Keith reported that one salesman he had been dealing with:

> is alright though, he said that he'd managed to make the 200 loaves (which he had previously been buying cheap per day) just by shorting his shops, it's easy, he's been going there for years, and they trust him . . . he did one shop for 42 loaves!

Some few salesmen, without access to these techniques, were forced to inflate legitimate orders, and back this with embarrassed claims that 'trade's picking up', and other hollow cheerinesses. To try and forestall the obvious cynicism, most of them added 'I know it looks bad, but trade really is picking up'. However, in the event, no salesmen were revealed outright at this stage. If all were not completely credible, at least all provided themselves with *some* defence.

The initial response of the salesmen was to react separately to the news (not because of differing work locations as was the case with the inside men, but because the salesmen drifted in singly some time between 2 and 7 p.m. after completing their rounds, and heard the news from different people at different times and in different ways) and, at first, form individual preliminary *inventories*. As with the inside men, there was a class of Innocent salesmen (1 out of 17 wholesale salesmen and about 19 out of 27 retail salesmen) who reacted to the news as if the occasion it reported was unique and, after asking 'what happened?' in a curious and uninvolved way, took no further part in the disaster. The rest, the Suspected salesmen, believed that confrontation with the management was inevitable, and almost immediately got together to prepare a collective response to any accusation.

The Wellbread's management on the other hand arranged a salesman's 'meeting' (in fact consecutive interviews) and attempted to exploit the collective preparation of the salesmen by spreading a nasty line. As Keith put it:

> Well, they had all the wholesalers in the office, one at a time, and put pressure on them, saying that Doug and me had told them everything . . . this was about bread, cake, biscuits, the lot . . . they said we'd been supplying them with everything, they said that I told them.

In the initial panic some salesmen believed that Keith had

'squealed'. One salesman, white with fear, told me before the meeting (I was able to reassure him) that 'they've got a list of times, dates, places and everything . . . Keith's apparently told them everything'. Of course, this pressure was backed with a subtly conveyed message that the management were prepared to treat informers leniently. One salesman reported after the 'meeting' that he had:

> never seen anything like it, I'd never been in there before, and we were in there 21 minutes, . . . he said that we must have known about it, and why didn't we do anything, he said that he knew all the information, and why didn't we [confess] cor! . . . I don't want to go in there again.

This form of attack is strong. Most of the men found that they believed that people in Keith's position usually 'squealed'. As Geoff the despatch man, put it:

> Blokes who are caught doing this sort of thing, generally will throw as much as they can at everybody in every direction, feeling at the time that the more muck they throw, they'll put what they've done in a brighter light.

On top of this, Eadley acted the part convincingly. He told me:

> We're very careful about who we accuse of anything . . . we knew something was going on, not because we were short of anything, most of the time the stock tied up alright, but because it developed into a pattern . . . it was very upsetting though, one of the lads had been with us a long time, and he was in a position of trust . . . what leaves a nasty taste in your mouth was that he'd been pointing the finger at others, not directly mind you, but he'd been trying to put it on to other blokes, he'd been coming to me and telling me things for some time . . . no names, no facts, just suspicions . . . but they got over-confident, see, that's how we caught them, they involved too many people, and we got all the facts about the one case involving the biscuits, and that was it, and it all came spilling out then! . . . he couldn't tell us enough.

Although, as it turned out, this was an incredible claim (nobody was apprehended on the basis of this alleged 'squeal', there were no signed statements of the sort produced by Alfred's 'shop'), it was widely believed. Those managers who knew about Keith's previous (and innocent) attempts to have something done about dealing now cited this as evidence that he was a known 'squealer'. Mr Morrisey said to the whole despatch shift 'I've heard it from several sources that Keith's been talking, that he's been saying that we're doing it as well . . . anyway, I know for a fact that Keith's been in there telling them that sort of thing before'. Similarly, most of the involved salesmen believed, as one put it, that 'heads are going to roll', because Keith had spilt the beans to the management.

However, the sales interviews did not, ultimately, reveal any hard empirical knowledge that Keith had said anything. The implication was there, but there were no facts to back it up. Pressure was put on salesmen, but no signed statements were put before them. At the same time, George and Lonny (the two wholesale salesmen who had had the biscuits) met Keith on the evening of the 21st, and, as George widely reported to the other salesmen, 'he hasn't said anything, he came round mine yesterday, and he swore that he hadn't said a thing to them, and that's good enough for me'.[18] What was good enough for George, was good enough for most of the other salesmen. As a result, after the interviews, as another salesman cheerily put it 'we're still here, yes, and they're still looking for Mr Big . . . The Godfather, they're still looking for him'. However, during the interviews two salesmen cracked under managerial pressure: Bert and Claude were both weak enough to turn informer. Keith takes up the story:

> Well, I think they was after trying to nail somebody big . . . they nailed two didn't they? . . . they had all the wholesalers in one at a time, and two of them cracked . . . who admitted they was taking the bread off Doug and me . . . from what I can make out, Eadley was going round saying 'This time I shall have Mr Big', this was what was worrying them last week, because he said he knew who Mr Big was, and, 'at 4, in 60 minutes' time, I shall have Mr Big in the net' . . . I don't know [who this Mr Big was], he thinks there was a ringleader, who was organising it all, that was the impression they was under, that there was a ringleader who was organising it all.

However, both Bert and Claude gave limited, backdated 'confessions' as corrupt*ee* dealees in small amounts – again, the management was only succeeding in extracting token admissions. Most importantly, the character of the 'talker' was again as corrupt*ee* – an acknowledgement of hierarchical organisational form, but simultaneously an implicit direction to seek the elusive 'Mr Big' amongst the inside men. This naturally took the heat off the salesmen, although what concluded impact and prompted *rescue* work was that during the interviews the management made a fatal slip, a crucial mistake, which at a stroke revealed their claims to current inside knowledge to be wholly fraudulent. As Keith put it:

> They made a vital mistake, see, because all the time, all the time they were having those blokes in, only once did they mention a price . . . of what they were buying this bread for, and they made a terrible mistake on the price, which afterwards, and all the wholesalers agreed, that that proved beyond any doubt that we wasn't guilty [of squealing] because they said 5/– a tray see? . . . he had all those wholesalers in, and he told them, he said: 'You've been buying bread at 5/– a tray' . . . course, as soon as he said that, they knew it wasn't true, but by the time he had those other two in again [Bert and Claude] they couldn't get to them, see, and they both cracked . . . and they said: 'Yes, we have been given bread' . . . he didn't quote a price to those two.

Ironically, it had thus been Basil whose greed in having the Dan-era price of 5/– per tray increased to 10/– which had caused so much rancour at the time, which saved the salesmen. Importantly, the mistake was not just incorrect, it was dated. It demonstrated not just a slip of the tongue, but hopeful bluffing with outdated knowledge. Dealing could now, in theory, restart safe in the knowledge that it could do so invisibly. One problem remained. It was still possible that Keith and Doug (who, having lost all, had nothing further to lose) could blow the whistle. What was the *remedy* for this? As I have already shown (page 68) Keith was concerned that he was being scapegoated for all the losses that had occurred since Dan's sacking, bitter that the management had failed to act on his earlier warnings, and upset that Eadley did nothing to fulfill his private promise to 'get the rest of them'. To a smaller degree, Doug was bitter at the connections that had always been (fatefully) drawn between him and his erring brother. However, their gradual but inevitable detachment from the social life of the bakery and their slow adjustment to the realities of the outcome provided the remedy. Whilst remaining an explosive possibility, their rather specialised knowledge of dealing lies dormant.

The remedy thus applied, dealer networks moved inexorably toward *recovery*. The salesmen's adjustments to the drying of illicit bread supply (detailed on page 79) are essentially temporary. The situation is *elastic* (rather than plastic): a return to the pre-enforcement dealer *status quo ante* is inevitable, as the pure economic pressures to recovery gradually increase. Within three weeks, dealing was back to normal.

(iii) AN EVENT POSSIBILITY: CRIME AND DEVIANCY AMPLIFICATION?

In the drama of the management's search for 'Mr Big', normal working life became critically abnormal, and things 'got out of hand'. But, were these real 'things' empirical or symbolic? Was it *events* which got out of hand, or *interpretations* of them?

To ask 'what happened' is to make an initial assumption that (after Thomas) a situation defined as real will be real in its consequences. But this only locates and does not resolve the debate. Were the real consequences of such definition empirical or symbolic? This distinction is not conventionally felt to be necessary. Cohen (1973, p. 24), for example, runs both together when he says:

> Deviance [disaster] models are circular and amplifying: the impact (deviance) is followed by a reaction which has the effect of increasing the subsequent warning and impact, setting up a feed back system.

Let us consider the naïve empiricist view first. Did control 'lead' to deviance? Did the exercise of control statistically increase the practice of 'crime'? Stated as plainly as this, the thesis is inadequate. When control is exercised at Wellbread's it *does* in fact sometimes 'work'.[19] Did, then, deviance 'lead' to control? Yet again, regrettably, the conventional criminological view is as generally inadequate as I have just shown the traditional labelling position to be: even labelling theory (for all its early radical pretensions) has not yet budgeted for the possible effectiveness of control. Control sometimes 'fails' (labelling); sometimes 'works' (criminology) – these possibilities are arranged in Fig. 3.3, below.

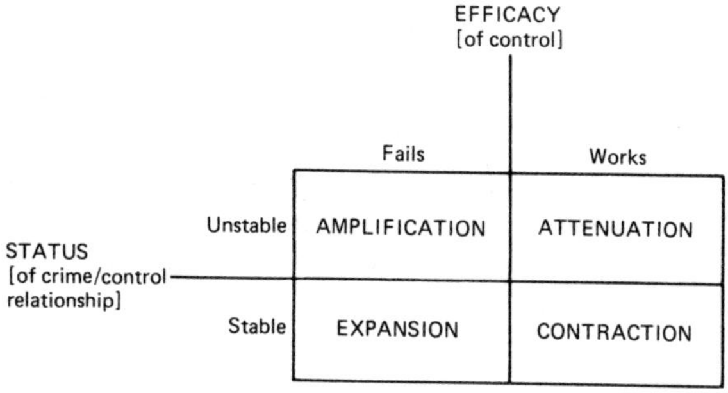

FIG. 3.3 *Control variations*

I have already described the sacking in some detail (and will pursue another part of an adequate analysis of it shortly); but first: how does it fit the control-wave model outlined in Chapter 2? Well, in the despatch department at Wellbread's, the control and practice of dealing revolves eternally in under-history eras which traditionally open and close with the exemplary sacking of a nominal number of participants.[20] The era of Keith and Douglas (as it is retrospectively known) began with the sacking of Dan, Doug's brother, a chargehand caught in cahoots with a salesman in 1970. The salesman had arranged for Dan to deal with his holiday relief, but the plan backfired (see note 8). Dan *and* the salesman were fired (breaking Smarteagh's Rule for the only time in living memory, although the salesman was reinstated later), thus propelling despatch life dramatically into the stage (see Fig. 2.8 on page 33 of Chapter 2) of 'more criminals caught'. As is customary at Wellbread's, most of the despatch crew were also dealing, but managerial investigations (as is also customary) merely revealed a few minor indiscretions. This was immediately followed by 'less crime': in other words, a full-blown CONTRAC-TION – in the terminology of the control-wave model.[21] This is not, of course, to say that 'less acts' took place. On the contrary, for the sake of both bakery appearances and customer appetites (the demand for each being somewhat inelastic), production runs were kept to full and usual strength, and white-overalled despatch men spent their nights, as usual, putting the usual amounts of bread on the salesmen's racks. There was a jittery air of unease, and some salesmen with cold feet in the bakery chose to warm them up by short-delivering their shops. There was as much crime about as there was weather: although the downpour at the bakery slowed to a drizzle complemented by occasional showers out on the rounds.[22] Donald, Dan's replacement, had been a roundsman and knew what would be, and indeed soon was, expected of him as despatch *major domo*. In the meantime, the control-wave moved into a slight and consequent period of ATTENUATION. No one else but Dan, and his opposite number in the sales team were caught, and control, after a bit of illusory tightening-up, lapsed to its usual apathetic state. This 'declining statistical basis for reaction against criminals' thus generated 'less action against criminals', and, as far as the managerial controllers were concerned, there was 'less crime'. But any satisfied smiles in the boardroom were immediately complemented by more satisfied smiles amongst the despatch night shift. The economic base of dealing remained constant, and Doug and Basil stepped in as major dealers until Donald, on the other shift, had learned the business. The Law of Increasing Criminals is not to be taken lightly. As I have already documented at length (see note 13), dealing gradually but inexorably dragged in the initially unwilling Keith. EXPANSION got under way and showed healthy productivity until nearly three years later, in February 1973, the management became aware yet again of 'more crime'.[23] 'More criminals caught' (Keith and Doug) provided 'increasing statistical basis for reaction against criminals', but AMPLIFICATION, in the guise of 'more action against criminals' was short-lived because of the critical managerial error of mis-pricing the tray price of 'hot' bread.[24] The Law of Diminishing Criminals (filtering through the managerial interviews) pushed the control-wave on to evidence of 'less crime' – as far as managerial controllers were concerned – with the recruitment of new dealers (Geoff, with the now experienced Donald) to satisfy the ever-present dealee demand.

The Keith and Douglas era was concluded, and the stage simultaneously set for the eventual slip-up and subsequent annihilation of the Geoff and Donald era.[25]

(iv) AN EVENT INTERPRETATION: CONTROL AND FANTASY TRANSLATION

However, control was not *wholly* without a separable and permanent effect, although, as we have just seen, it did not merely impinge on the dealing situation in a simplistic, non-reactive empirical way. In brief, while control did not simply catch criminals, it *did* provide some new 'evidence' to support managerial ideas about dealing. In this final section I shall try to show that life is more complex even than this, and that it is the very *provision* of evidence which is simultaneously the *generation* of evidence. 'Mr Big' and 'The Godfather' were *made*, and not found. Put simply, control translated fantasy into reality.

In assessing 'what happened', we are obliged to confess that nothing empirical or substantive occurred, and that the impact of control was purely a change in the conjoint symbolic construction of the event. Control changed the *interpretation* of the event, and not its empirical base: its *meaning* rather than its objective nature. So, in spite of the lack of any evidence naïvely supporting the unmodified deviancy-amplification thesis, there *is* evidence to support the quite separate (although conventionally merged)[26] fantasy-translation thesis.

I am suggesting that whilst control 'worked' empirically (albeit for a short while only), it simultaneously worked – but in a different way – symbolically. The management did not *discover* 'Mr Big' or 'The Godfather' – they *developed* them in the drama of control and enforcement. The 'search' for the two characters was, in other words, a self-fulfilling prophecy.[27] Before control action started neither character 'existed' other than as fantasy roles in suspicious managerial minds.

Consider Thomas's dictum again: If men define situations as real, they will be real in their consequences. Definitions are just definitions. Making them 'stick' requires a different sort of 'stick' – power. The more powerful the definer, the 'realer' the consequences. If power is sufficiently unequally distributed, then the definitions of the powerful may wholly eclipse those of the powerless. Now, this is precisely what happened at Wellbread's. For various reasons (not least among them being the superior position of the management) shop-floor 'theories' about what was 'happening' never seriously competed with the managerial formulation. It was not so much that the searches for the 'shopper' or the 'squealer' did not in theory compete with the search for the 'dealer', but rather that, in practice, they were not allowed to. The searches for the 'shopper' and the 'squealer' were soon driven underground and made private. Gradually the whole workforce conceded that the search for 'Mr Big' and 'The Godfather' was of pre-eminent public concern.

Conventional theory is not sympathetic to this issue. The basic conceptual proposition is the self-fulfilling prophecy.[28] As Merton (1968, p. 477) puts it, reflexivity is a basic property of the social (as strictly opposed to the natural) world, and:

> Public definitions of a situation (prophesies or predictions) become an integral part of the situation and thus affect subsequent developments.

Now, one of the more aesthetically pleasing perversities of social logic is the feedback of prediction on outcome. A nicely timed, placed and backed prophecy can be remarkably effective. Merton (*ibid*, p. 477) again:

> The self-fulfilling prophesy is, in the beginning, a *false* definition of the situation evoking a new behaviour which makes the originally false conception come *true*.

In a bank-run, for example, the rumour of insolvency creates the result of insolvency: everybody individually attempting to avoid a disaster collectively creates it.[29] Now, it *can* occur that two parties to an interaction can become involved in the separate production of groundless theories about each other, to which the other's actions (ironically a response to one's false definitions) provide a 'spurious' (in Merton's sense) verification. This produces a (theoretically endless) spiral of theoretical misconceptions and empirical confirmations, such as those documented by Laing *et al.* (1966).

This self-fulfilling prophecy possibility has been recast ably by Young (1971, p. 197) as a series of interactions (in his case, between police 'controllers' and 'deviant' drugtakers) which ultimately and ironically translate fantasy into reality. The two sets of self-fulfilling prophecy are, firstly, that of the controller (Young, 1971, pp. 196–7):

> Thus false theories are evolved and acted upon in terms of a social reaction, the result of which are changes, which, although merely a *product* of these theories, are taken by many to be a proof of their initial presumptions.

The deviants act equally perversely. Young continues:

> Similarly, the drugtaker, evolving theories as to the repressive nature of the police, finds them progressively proven as the gravity of the situation escalates.

Expressed diagrammatically (derived and improved from Young, 1971, p. 197), the dual model looks as follows (given in Fig. 3.4, below). Life at Wellbread's was not as conveniently

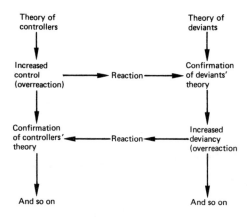

FIG. 3.4 *Double mutual fantasy-translation circuit*

neat and tidy as this. It was not that the workers (despatch men and salesmen) did not (like the management) have 'theories' about what had 'happened' but rather that, whereas the actions of the workers were crucial to the management's theory, the workers' theories were concerned with themselves (with miscreants within their *own* ranks) and not with the actions of management.

Young's model is of a *mutual* fantasy-translation circuit. For my purposes, a single fantasy-translation circuit (given in Fig. 3.5, page 90) is sufficient. This relatively formal treatment can now be applied to Wellbread's (Fig. 3.6, page 91) where the formal circuit is serialised. It may be now empirically conceived as an interpretive structure superimposed upon (but partly constitutive of) the control-waves already mentioned.

The paradoxical search-for/creation-of the 'dealer' encompas-

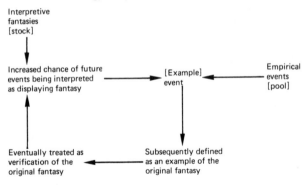

FIG. 3.5 *Single mutual fantasy-translation circuit*

sed seven separate stages of fantasy-translation. The stages of
Selection, Distortion, Search, Settlement, Retrospection, Propaganda, and finally of Indoctrination, gradually (culminating in
the 'spurious' delusion of the two offenders) convinced *everybody*
that the search had 'found' the folk devils. Like flying saucers
(Buckner, 1968, p. 227), 'Mr Big' and 'The Godfather' became a
Rorschach blot for the suddenly emergent fears of the work group.
As Buckner (*ibid*, p. 224) continues, 'this concrete name defined a
previously undefined class of phenomena and people began fitting
their experiences to it'. I'll describe the stages that this process
took at Wellbread's.

A basic occupational problem for salesmen is low wages. One
solution to this – dealing – also gives the inside men a bit extra.
Naturally, this provides an endless stream of events, deals, which
would be problematic if visible to management. For the management's part, most of this is concealed. Previous experience,
however, prompts them to be alert for any signs of (as they see it) a
sudden outburst of dealing. Dealing, routine for the men, is seen
as purely episodic by management. Accordingly, the single biscuit theft, and the emergence of Keith and Doug as culprits, was
in fact the SELECTION and misperception by the management
of one event from a series, and simultaneously the first stage in the
almost total evisceration and mutilation of its meaning.[30]

As the management moved to act, the second stage, that of
initial DISTORTION, emerged in the process of inventory-
taking. Here, the management's fairly crude interpretative fantasy stock was piously and petulantly consulted, and the pure
control fantasy form of dealing was picked out and speculatively

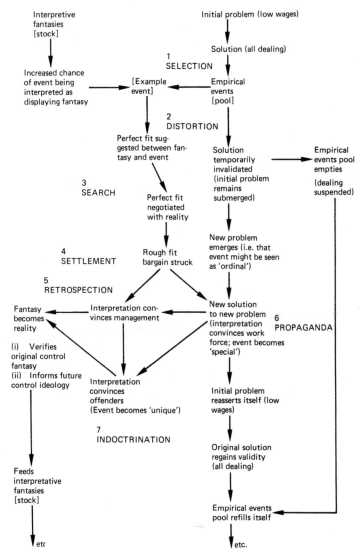

FIG. 3.6 *Fantasy translation: the creation of 'Mr Big' and 'The Godfather'*

matched with the event in question. The preferred outcome at this
stage was to define the offenders (Keith and Doug) as the
unwilling puppets dancing to the tune of an about-to-be-named
'brain'.

Having selected the 'ring' fantasy, the next step was to SEARCH the suddenly visible reality in order to prise the arch instigator from his lair. Fitting fantasies to reality involves negotiations with those simultaneously involved in its joint production. The interviews which the management conducted with the despatch men and the salesmen can thus be conceived as attempts to fill out the stereotype with a real person, and justify the original selection of the 'ring' fantasy.

As I have documented, the search was surprisingly unsuccessful, merely unearthing a few coy confessions which, far from belittling and overshadowing Keith and Doug's role in events, in fact magnified them. This was a problem. Fantasies cannot be sustained in total contradiction to the evidence. On the other hand, the management was not prepared to capitulate entirely. A review of their fantasy stock at this stage produced an acceptable SETTLEMENT – the lesser 'rotten apple' fantasy. Attaching this label to the event was a lot more satisfactory both for the management (who could now 'clear' the event) and for the men, who could subsequently resume life as usual.

The striking of this bargain (together with some face-saving and loss-recovery work) allowed the management to practise a little self-indulgent RETROSPECTION. They became self-congratulatory (not naïvely that they had been right all along, but) because they had been astute and flexible enough to switch fantasy horses midstream (and without losing direction – 'ring' and 'rotten apple' fantasies share the trait of hierarchical organisation), and lucky enough to be faced with less of a problem than they had initially supposed. The original control theory was thus roughly substantiated, and this would no doubt subsequently function as a good empirical reason for initially supposing the worst the next time 'something happened'.

To a certain degree, this feeling functioned widely as PROPAGANDA. The men also found this outcome satisfactory, but for different reasons. Their acceptance that the event was 'special' allowed it to be removed from the mainstream of despatch and sales routine (where it was inconveniently blocking 'normal' dealing), pigeonholed, catalogued, shelved and pushed to one side where it could harmlessly be assured of a permanent place as a milestone in the unofficial under-history of the bakery.[31] Of course (now that the management could be persuaded to relax their awkward scrutiny) normal dealing could resume invisibly.

We now reach the ultimate, and in many ways the most curious and paradoxical stage in the creative discovery of 'Mr Big' and 'The Godfather'. Whilst the negotiated and subtle managerial fantasy propagandised the workforce, it worked as INDOCTRI-NATION on the two men concerned. Eventually Keith and Doug came to believe *themselves* that they *were* some sort of 'Mr Big' or 'The Godfather'! Keith in particular began to see himself as Wellbread's answer to the Great Train Robbers, recalling, some time after the occasion, that:

It was never intended to be an organisation really, although I suppose partly that was my fault, as I always class myself as having a fairly organised mind ... you know, like the great biscuit robbery, that was quite carefully planned, and quite cleverly executed, we just made one fatal mistake, we took a man with us we couldn't trust.[32]

NOTES

1. Apart from 2 weeks of participant observation in 1971 (one in August, and one at Christmas), all the observation fell between June 1972 and May 1973. I worked a total of 24 weeks (6 months) in the despatch department in full weeks. As well as this, I worked for 19 separate days (totalling nearly 3 weeks) there, on odd occasions as a casual employee. This provided 9 weeks of night work (usually a 61-hour week), and 13 weeks of days (a 67-hour week). Apart from the 2 weeks in 1971, I worked for 18 complete weeks in 1972 (11 consecutive weeks from 4 June to 25 August; 1 week in both September and November, two in October, and the remaining three in December) and 9 odd days, mostly in November. In 1973 I worked two full weeks in April, and 10 extra days spread evenly from Christmas to May.

2. I interviewed 11 despatch workers (10 men and 1 woman) mostly at their homes on weekday afternoons when they were on night shift, between 7 January and 23 May 1973. I conducted a total of 19 taped and transcribed interviews – a total of 22 hours and 35 minutes (and 225 typed foolscap pages). The average interviewee was interviewed for 2 hours, producing 20 pages of verbatim typescript. In fact, interviews varied considerably. The maximum was for 5 hours and 10 minutes (48 pages) and the minimum was for only 1 hour (and 7 pages). Five interviewees were interviewed once only; 5 suffered 2 interviews, and one man talked to me on 4 separate occasions.

3. 'Dealing' (wherein despatch men sell bread which doesn't belong to them to the salesmen) is treated at length in Ditton (1977, pp. 105–13), and shortly in note 11 below. The sacking took place on 20 February 1973. By then I had finished most of the participant observation (and only worked for 2 complete weeks, and 8 separate days afterwards), but had only completed 5 out of an eventual 19 interviews.

4. See Baker and Chapman (eds) (1962); Fritz (1961); and Pine (1974).

5. He (1973, p. 23) declares that (i) the sequence has not been empirically established for social disasters, (ii) in social disasters, the stages should be consequentially and not merely sequentially related, (iii) crucially, with social disasters, the event does not occur independently of its reaction. Whilst natural models are linear and constant, social models are circular and amplifying (I shall address this possibility later).

6. And is informed by the 'scapegoat studies'; i.e.: Bucher (1957); Drabeck and Quarantelli (1967); Quarantelli (1955); Veltfort and Lee (1943).

7. The salesman involved in this previous big deal, Lonny, was also involved in this one. His punishment then (in accordance with Smarteagh's Rule: roughly, (in any case) salesmen are innocently corrupted by bent inside men, see p. 78, above) was temporary suspension on full pay, and then eventual reinstatement to both licit and illicit sales life.

8. A renewed possibility. Despatch history is characterised by 'eras' culminating in control-waves and sackings. The previous era-change was brought about by the sacking of Dan, Doug's brother. Keith explained: 'Dan got it for putting trays of bread on the rounds, and he got caught with "X", apparently there was "Y" went on "X"'s round, and "X" said to Dan: "He's alright", and he told "Y" the same, "If you want any bread, see Dan" . . . he supplied him with bread all the week, and then on Saturday morning, Dan gave him his bread, and they nobbled him, "Y" shopped him and he was out the same as Doug and I, instant dismissal'.

9. Biscuits have a long pedigree as a highly thievable item at Wellbread's. Doug told me 'it first started when everyone used to go and get their own biscuits, the biscuit store was always left open, must have been about five years ago . . . well, we used to get what we wanted for ourselves, and then a particular bloke said he could get rid of a bit of stuff . . . he weren't actually on the rounds . . . things sort of started from there'.

10. This notices the way that management use words like 'pilferage' and 'fiddling' as *generic* as well as *specific* descriptions.

11. (See note 10). The only type of illicit theft we are talking about here is 'dealing' (Ditton, 1977, ch. 4). Dealing has two structurally necessary *Roles* (Deal*er* and Deal*ee*), but under different organisational regimes (structures) these can emerge clothed in different *Characters*. For example, firstly, as 'Hierarchic' where one of the role-fillers is seen as the corrupt*or*, and the other as the corrupt*ed* (a moral characterisation); and secondly, 'Democratic' where character faithfully reflects and neutrally reports role, with dealer and dealee becoming just seller and buyer (a technical characterisation).

12. There are good reasons why enforcers typically choose the 'ring' fantasy in the control of illicit activities involving a number of participants. The concept of a 'leader' is less morally threatening than the alternative conception that the majority of practitioners are willingly engaging in deviant acts (as Bunyan, 1976, p. 137 *et passim* shows, this is increasingly likely for increasingly serious crimes). Also, as a control *ideology*, it pragmatically fits available control mechanisms particularly well. The idea that one or two individuals can take the moral and legal blame for all the participants nicely fits the usual empirical case where enforcers can only catch one or two practitioners. If they can be made to take the blame for all the misbehaviour,

then the enforcers' honour is satisfied, and the offence seems 'cleared'. However, should many practitioners fall into enforcement hands, there may be no need for the 'ring' fantasy (or at least no need for the 'leader' illusion). Although the police refused to acknowledge the Mr Big nonsense in the Great Train Robbery, Peta Fordham, a journalist, couldn't resist it. She refers (1965, p. 25) to a 'mind' or to the 'brain', and continues: 'The original idea of a mail train robbery was thought out by a highly intelligent man who was (and still is) an uncrowned intellectual king of the underworld'. Even the participants deny this spurious hierarchical imputation, and suggest a democratic reality. Ronald Biggs (quoted in McIntosh, 1971, p. 124) claims: 'There have been suggestions, even positive claims, that a "Mr Big" or "The Mind" was the brain behind the robbery. This is sheer nonsense. The plan was formulated from the knowledge contributed by the men who made up the "train gang". The meetings which were held to discuss the business were usually conducted by Reynolds and Edwards, but everybody made suggestions, which were either accepted or rejected, usually on a show of hands'.

13. The hand of irony touched many in this control-wave, fingering Keith as much as anybody else. In fact his latter career at Wellbread's is an almost perfect example of the fantasy-translation model (introduced at the end of this chapter). For many years Keith had never dealt, although latterly, at holiday times if there was any spare bread (which would have otherwise gone to waste), he had given it away. He remembers, 'I just said to him, George that is, "There's a 100 loaves there, if you want them, take them", and he took them, and I never thought no more about it . . . anyway, *after* the holiday, he . . . gave me a fiver . . . I said: "What's this for?", and he said: "For the bread you gave me before Christmas" and then: "You look after me, and I'll look after you" . . . well, after that, if I had some bread over, I used to give it to him'. At a later date, after Keith had checked the salesmen's racks one morning and finding a lot of 'extra' bread on, he was about to check them again when 'Douglas came sidling over, and he said to me: "What are you doing then?", so I said "I'm now going to check the rounds", so he said "You know we're making a pound", so I said: "I didn't, Doug" . . . but they'd got me a little bit by the goolies, see, because I admit that I had, in the past, given George bread, you see? . . . and he said: "You know we're making a pound, and you're making a pound and all, you leave us alone, and we'll leave you alone". . . . I said "What do you mean? I'm not making anything", and he said "You're a bloody fool then, you'd best come in with us" . . . I was absolutely shocked, I didn't realise what was going on'. As Doug put it 'one day, Keith found some bread on the rounds . . . and we thought "Oh, well, we'd better bring him in as well"'. Keith did *not* immediately join in. He remembers 'What I did was to think about it very carefully, and I went to Fadley, and I told him, I didn't give him any names, I didn't shop anybody, that was my job, and being as I was foreman of despatch, it was my job to see that it doesn't happen . . . but he didn't believe me, he just didn't believe me, he said 'You give me the names, and the places, and whatnot"!' This failure to act was compounded by what happened three days later. As Keith put it 'They had a roundsman for fiddling, his books were short and everything, and he told them the whole story, he named everybody . . . how much they were paid, and everything'.

But no real action was taken. As Doug put it 'That didn't change things really . . . just, for a fortnight, they had a purge on'. Keith then warned the despatch men that 'if I caught anybody, I'd shop them, I was prepared to go into the office and testify, and that was a warning, and that should have been good enough [Keith then caught a roundsman with two trays of extra] but they [management] wouldn't listen, they wouldn't listen to me, and they wouldn't listen to Morrisey, for some reason, Sales covered it up'. Thoroughly disillusioned, Keith, not really knowing what to do, eventually decided to solve the problem himself, and subsequently closed dealing. Fairly soon, Basil and Doug began to deal extra behind Keith's back. When Keith discovered this, in fury, he again tried to stop dealing. However, Basil soon approached him, and 'he said "I'm in trouble", and I said "What's the matter?", and he said "I can't manage, I'm really getting in financial trouble, I been used to having all this money for so long now, and I'm up a gum tree", and he said "We know quite a bit about you, which could put you in trouble"'. On top of this, Keith was approached by 'several of the wholesalers, who said "You can't stop it just like that" because it'll raise such suspicion, if everybody orders more bread, there'll be all hell let loose, they'll want to know what the hell's going on'. Finally, mostly in order to *organise, control* and therefore *cover* the amounts dealt, Keith capitulated and joined Basil and Doug.

14. In 1962, In Atlanta Penitentiary, Vito Genovese, serving a 15-year stretch for drug smuggling (incorrectly) suspected a fellow inmate Joseph Valachi, of informing. Valachi, believing himself to be thus a marked man, killed a fellow inmate under the (erroneous) assumption that he was an assassin. To avoid the death penalty for *this* killing, Valachi finally 'talked' (Talese, 1971, p. 124).

15. Both names selected from the current British fantasy stock. 'Mr Big' has a long British pedigree (see McIntosh, 1971, p. 124) and 'The Godfather' comes from the recent Mario Puzo book of the same name. Both epithets were wheeled out to do faithful service yet again in the media coverage of the Bertie Smalls gang bank robberies (Ball *et al.*, 1978, p. 139).

16. Keith later felt that second thoughts could be wisely replaced by third ones. 'It's silly really, my father-in-law was saying tonight, "you should have told them to go and get a real policeman, and you would have talked to him", but when I was in there, I didn't think really, probably, come to think about it, they probably didn't have enough evidence to take us to court anyway'.

17. This would have been 'squealing' if the short and curly misdemeanours by which the informant is held are the same as those which he ultimately reveals. Alfred's offence was quite different to Keith's and Doug's; he only knew about Keith and Doug by chance and not by participation.

18. Keith also managed to convince George and Lonny that he might yet still do so, although £25 (duly received) would buy his silence on the issue of George and Lonny's complicity.

19. See, e.g., Hall *et al.* (1978, p. 184) and Scull (1972, p. 284) and especially Ross, Campbell and Glass (1970).

20. Control, as soon as it is exercised, loses its impulse value, and it is unusual for more than two participants to be caught (see, for example, the clean-up campaign reported in Ditton, 1972, fn. 81, p. 56.) The effect of control is

'exemplary' – in other words, those apprehended are severely punished as an *example* to the rest of the 'gang'.

21. The 'total' population of the despatch department was 11 (manager, two chargehands and 8 operatives). Naturally, they were all doing 'acts' – giving salesmen bread – which could be interpreted as dealing. Only Rob Siddell could personally claim to be 'falsely accused' if so labelled. But the 'criminal' population, as revealed by control, only numbered 2: Keith and Doug; and as far as they were concerned, dealing then stopped [although we 'know' better]. A nice comparative example has recently been offered by Ball *et al.* (1978, p. 154). Commenting upon the successful conviction of Bertie Smalls and his friends and accomplices, they tell us:

> In terms of crime statistics the efforts of the Robbery Squad had proved highly successful. Not only had some of the most formidable robbers of the decade been put away, but the fact of their conviction provided a powerful disincentive for would-be imitators. The number of bank robberies within the London area fell from sixty-five in 1972 to twenty-six in the following year.

Those who believe in 'dark figures' also believe that bank robberies are less likely to go unreported than, say, abortions or (in Scotland) homosexual acts (see Hood and Sparks 1970, Fig. 1b). But a low probability is not qualitatively distinguishable from a high one. With the Robbery Squad now turning its eye elsewhere, no doubt Smalls and Co. (upon expiry of sentence) – or youthful imitators – will be back in business.

22. Let me review a terminological ambiguity at this point. In Chapter 2 I claimed that it was inappropriate to talk of 'crimes' being 'committed' before a properly and legally constituted court had permanently delivered its verdict. Yet, here, in Chapter 3, I have referred to 'dealing' and 'theft', and to the 'Guilty' and the 'Innocent'. Unravelling this apparent contradiction depends upon clarifying what it makes sense to say *under the appropriate circumstances.* The discrepancy arises out of analysing control 'societally' (in Chapter 2), and crime 'situationally' (in Chapter 3). Situationally, it is allowable common-sensically to assess observed events in terms of the meanings attributed to those events by the actors involved. Thus, commonsensically (and for some practical purposes), Keith and Doug were situationally guilty. At the societal level, however (tackled in Chapter 2), it is only legitimate to claim, in analysing the empirical material reviewed here, that a 'mistake' has occurred in the issuing of bread – or biscuits – and that this like *any* other 'act' (*pace* Wittgenstein) may eventually emerge as theft through the application of control. Indeed, I have tried to show at the beginning of this chapter that 'mistakes' are a universal problem for despatch operatives, and it is precisely the potential that control possesses to elevate these to 'crimes' which makes despatch life so anxious.

23. Their awareness of 'crime' is fortuitous rather than planned.

24. AMPLIFICATION is technical here, and denuded of social corollaries. No Wilkins-type 'progressive detachment loop' [see note 6, Fig. 2.1a, Chapter 2] was set in train for the rest of the despatch employees. Industrial relations are tiresome enough without engendering additional alienation among, and

isolation of, employees. On the other hand, for Keith and Douglas a 'total detachment' programme was involved. Thus, for neither the Guilty nor the Innocent did mutual social relations become progressively strained.

25. Natural and social progression has (I understand) prevented those particular individuals from playing their expected role in the next control-wave. Wally has retired (with Donald being promoted to despatch manager), and Geoff is now dead: an industrial casualty of a different sort.

26. Young (1971, pp. 189–97) usually fails to distinguish the two processes, and this is also true of a recent, and otherwise excellent book on mugging (Hall *et al.*, 1978), wherein both deviance amplification and fantasy-translation are portrayed as 'spirals' (*ibid*, p. 76), whereas, from my perspective, the latter is a circuit. In another recent book (on drug cultures) Willis (1978) has claimed that an empirical mixing (rather than separation) of drug-users and drug-controllers has produced reality-confirmation rather than fantasy-translation. he says (*ibid*, p. 122):

> That the controllers may have a critical account of what motivates the 'deviants' is not really germane, if they do have a mode of cultural contact, if they can play out a relevant internal cultural rule for the 'deviant' group. It is not surprising that agents of social control should legitimate their institutionally controlled objectives by criticism of the 'deviant' but this theoretical knowledge need not prevent a complex *modus vivendi* developing between the control agency and the deviant group which does not imply automatic deterioration and hostility of relations.

Another interesting use of the fantasy-translation model has been made by Armstrong and Wilson (1973, pp. 86, 88).

27. The search for the *Shopper* may be another example of this process. However, I have no evidence to support such a claim (even less to support any claim that the failure to find a *Squealer* was a similar self-fulfilling prophecy) and to admit this is no confession of inadequate data as I have only been concerned with *Shoppers* and *Squealers* in so far as they affected the search for the *Dealer*.

28. Two alternatives are: firstly, the *'suicidal prophecy'* (Merton, 1968, fn. 1, p. 477) 'which so alters human behaviour from what would have been its course had the prophesy not been made, that it fails to be borne out' (a false description leads to new behaviour which proves the definition incorrect) and secondly, (Davis and Olesen, 1970, fn. 10, p. 98) the *'self-negating prophecy'* (a true definition leads to new behaviour which proves the definition incorrect). I would suggest a third, the *self-denying prophecy* (a false definition encourages repeated behaviour which fails to prove the definition incorrect). For example, Engels (1845, p. 143) recalls that, in 19th-century England, sickly children were given laudanum in the hope of a cure. Laudanum actually makes them worse, but their worsened condition is seen as a result of insufficient medication. They are then given laudanum in increasing doses until they die (of it).

29. A nice example of professional self-fulfillment is given in Balk (1962). 'Block-busters' (unscrupulous real-estate dealers) make money by inexorably advancing the house-ownership colour line against the wishes of *all* white vendors. Whites sell cheap to avoid living in a black neighbourhood,

and blacks buy dear to get a foothold in a white one. In trying to avoid a personal disaster, fleeing white owners create a general one.

30. This is not really gratuitous scapegoating, which is (Klapp, 1959, p. 72) the displacement of blame on the *wrong* people, but rather, *exampling* (see Ditton, 1972, pp. 43–5) which leaves the victim the feeling of unfairness without any public grounds for talking about it.

31. Medalia and Larsen (1958) show that it is collectively easier to deal with an event if it can be assimilated to a cause regarded as episodic or transient ('the only example' of 'greed'), and if it may be narrowly focused (two men) in a way that both absorbs vague threats and allows something to be done (sacking).

32. Naturally enough, Keith's failure to identify with this stereotype whilst still at work *and* his later self-explanatory embracement of it are related to his initial access to a pool of justifying motives through participation in the culture of 'part-time crime' (see Ditton, 1977, esp. Ch. 4), and his subsequent withdrawal from that culture (and its attendant vocabulary of rationalisation) provided by his sacking.

4 'Responsibility' v. Response Ability: The Controlological Programme

What I tried to establish in Chapter 2 was that it is technically intellectually improper for anyone to claim that a 'crime' has been 'committed' until a properly constituted court has delivered that verdict as final. This now needs slight comparative qualification. I am not suggesting that individuals cannot *intend* to break the law. Nor that *situational* ethnographic work designed to display and intellectually organise those intentions in writing (e.g., Ditton, 1977) is now to be declared faulty, defunct, and all-along-misguided and henceforth-to-be-recanted.[1] What I am suggesting is that at the level of *societally* theorised ethnography, those intentions are unimportant and wholly insignificant when compared with the intentions of the infinitely more powerful controllers.[2] What universally decides whether or not a person is 'guilty' is the eventual finding of the court – something only probabilistically associated with his (or anybody else's) claims concerning his initial intent.

One crucial implication of this approach, developed in Chapter 3, given now that control rather than 'crime' is the vital element, is that explanations of the rise or fall in crime rates have to be sought elsewhere than in the motives and intentions of those eventually called 'criminal'. Naturally, this transforms the question of whether or not control 'works' or 'fails' into an inherently tautological one: one where the outcome of control activity can be traced to the nature of that control activity. In other words, the issue is *not* that control 'works' or 'fails' in the sense that people (e.g., despatch workers) cease to 'do acts', but rather that it is within the nature of control that its particular simple exercise is guaranteed to produce the *evidence* of success or failure. In the case of the despatch workers, as I pointed out in Chapter 3, bread was dutifully heaved on to the salesmen's racks after the sacking in a way behaviourally identical to that 'done' before.[3] It is not even clear that situational meanings underwent a transformation from typical dishonesty to episodic honesty at the time. Although understandably leery despatch workers took greater care than usual to minimise the chances of unfortunate apprehension for making a 'mistake', what is critical is that, as far as they are concerned, the power to alter or make such decisions lies exclusively elsewhere. In the (analyst's) vernacular: whether or not 'crimes' were 'committed' depended upon the management. So I am not claiming that the despatch workers or the salesmen did not *take* extra precautions during this period (in fact, they did): rather that such activity on their part was relatively pointless. If control had wanted them, it could have had any or all of them. But that was manifestly not the managerial point. Although entrapment did *not* spread, this was unrelated to the protective strategies performed by those at risk (i.e., the whole workforce). The small spread of control was related instead to the commercially careful designs and intentions of the 'controllers' – the management. It would have helped them little to 'discover' (an outcome which the exercise of control could have produced independently) that everybody was 'doing it' – as, in the purely situational sense, they were. Sacking one workforce and then replacing it with another is merely expensive in recruitment and training. Doing so under unchanged managerial circumstances merely presents a new set of workers with an old set of work problems and constraints. The new men will simply make the old 'mistakes'. If the intention is to leave the situation unchanged, then it is commercially fruitless (although possibly morally satisfactory) to dispense with the existing, experienced, and expensively trained men. After all, their propensity to make 'mistakes' is part of the work situation, rather than of their own (in)abilities. No, the essence of managerial strategy is divide and rule. The supreme form for its achievement is exemplary disciplining, the success of which is guaranteed by retaining the *rest* of the workforce, together with their memories of what can (arbitrarily) happen.[4] This 'exampling' does not occur because losses, of any imagined or defined variety, have passed some magically formulated limit of managerial tolerance; it occurs instead when, simply, unsolicited information that some otherwise unaccountable losses may be pinned on a small section of the workforce coincides with the managerial definition (put crudely) that in the eternal round of work discipline 'it is time we made an example of somebody'.

Now, one implication of these remarks is that a theory of control is required which can be formulated and understood quite independently of any, henceforth dependent, theory of crime.[5] In other words the issue at hand in this use of ethnographic data is one of societal *response ability*, rather than one of situational and individual *'responsibility'*. This recommendation is deduced in the light of the failure of both conventional criminological theory and of the traditional labelling perspective to spell out the basis for such a programme: something itself derived, as I suggested in Chapter 1, from the failure of followers of labelling to liberate themselves from the inferential structures laid down by positivist criminology. In fact, even if an unholy alliance could be forged temporarily between conventional criminology and traditional labelling, it could not satisfactorily account for the full range of empirically discovered and theoretically possible crime-control relationships. Considering Fig. 4.1, below,[6] whilst neither conventional

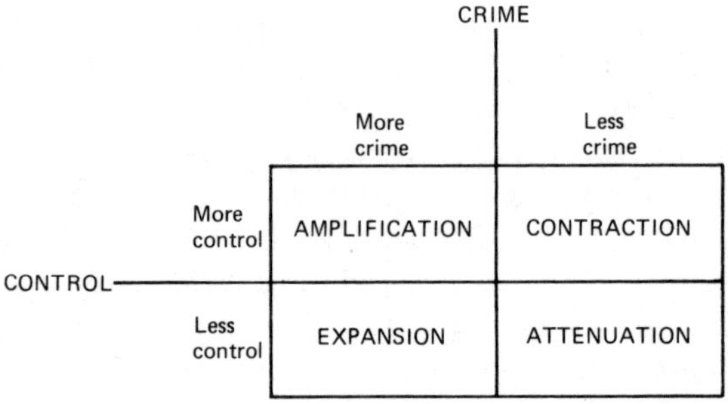

		CRIME	
		More crime	Less crime
CONTROL	More control	AMPLIFICATION	CONTRACTION
	Less control	EXPANSION	ATTENUATION

FIG. 4.1 *Response Ability*

criminological theorists nor followers of the labelling perspective would necessarily deny the validity of any of the four possibilities outlined, the former gather chiefly around the idea that crime leads to control (by empirically observing either contraction,[7] or, more usually, expansion);[8] and the latter around the obverse premise that control leads to crime (by working with instances of amplification,[9] or, occasionally, of attenuation).[10] The hiatus

grows because neither camp contains an adequate theory on its
own terms to account for the empirical observations of the other.
It is this gap, of course, that controlology is designed to fill.[11]

It is not that control hasn't been studied to date (in fact, quite
the reverse), but rather that those studies have emphasised
situational aspects to the neglect of societal considerations. Scull
(1977, pp. 7, 8; latter emphasis added) puts it like this:

> Certainly a considerable literature now exists on control agen-
> cies, including studies of the police and the criminal justice
> system, prisons, agencies for the blind, and hospitals for the
> mentally retarded and the mentally ill. Although some were
> written before the rise of labelling theory, the bulk of these
> studies were done in the 1960s and were more or less explicitly
> guided by the societal reaction perspective. But the issue is no
> longer the question of *whether* the agencies have been subjected
> to sociological scrutiny (though even the strongest critics of the
> societal reaction approach would concede its contribution in
> making this initial step); it is, rather, the *adequacy* of that
> scrutiny. And here the perspective's defenders are on much
> weaker ground.
>
> Existing literature on control agencies focuses primarily on
> 'the direct impact on the processed deviants of organisational
> settings and programs'. Attention tends to be narrowly fixed on
> the role of the agencies in selecting and processing the deviant
> population, with particular interest in how their activities in
> these respects serve to redefine and remake the identity of
> individual deviants . . . it is this which led to the overriding
> concern with deviant identity *and to the crucial but as yet only
> partially liberating notion of control as an independent factor* in shaping
> and producing deviance.

Equally regrettably (as I mentioned in Chapter 1) the immediate reaction to this trend – epitomised in *The New Criminology*
(Taylor, Walton and Young, 1973) – errs in the opposite direction, but is equivalently narrow in scope. But where *The New
Criminology* may be faulted for dogmatically deducing the nature
of control from a challengeable interpretation of selected parts of
Marx's work, a recent work, *Policing the Crisis* (Hall *et al.*, 1978)
has instead induced a pragmatic analysis of control in current
British society based *not* on ideas of a 'rising crime rate' (conven-

tional criminology), nor upon structurally limited symbolic interactionist conceptions like moral entrepreneur (traditional labelling),[12] but rather from a close empirical analysis of the development of British society since the end of the 1940s, based on the idea of an emergent hegemonic crisis which gave birth in the early 1970s to what the authors refer to as 'law-and-order society'. Interestingly (in terms of the analysis given here), they see the latter, analytically, as (Hall *et al.*, 1978, p. 122), 'a "mapping together" of moral panics into a *general panic* about social order'. One of the values of their approach is that it is capable of repairing the original analysis of moral panics precisely on the lines suggested by Scull.[13] For example, Hall *et al.* (*ibid*, p. 221) comment:

> The problem concerns the relation to our analysis – which is pitched at the level of the state apparatus and the maintenance of forms of hegemonic domination – of the phenomenon described earlier as the *moral panic*. The concepts of 'state' and 'hegemony' appear, at first sight, to belong to different conceptual territory from that of the 'moral panic'. And part of our intention is certainly to situate the 'moral panic' as one of the forms of appearance of a more deepseated historical crisis, and thereby to give it greater historical and theoretical specificity. This re-location of the conception at a different and deeper level of analysis does not, however, lead us to abandon it altogether as useless. Rather, it helps us to identify the 'moral panic' as one of the principal surface manifestations of the crisis, and in part to explain how and why the crisis came to be *experienced* in that form of consciousness, and what the displacement of a conjunctural crisis into the popular form of a 'moral panic' accomplishes, in terms of the way the crisis is managed and contained. We have therefore retained the notion of the 'moral panic' as a necessary part of our analysis: attempting to redefine it as one of the key ideological forms in which a historical crisis is 'experienced and fought out'.

However, although the authors of *Policing the Crisis* have added significantly to our historical understanding of moral panics (or control-waves), they have formulated little in the way of 'theoretical specificity'. This is precisely the sense in which the argument in Chapter 2 here might be said to dovetail with their concerns, and function as a complementary and critical footnote to their analysis. Further, by showing that control-waves have an endogenous and self-completing cyclical logic, it is possible to deduce that whilst they may be dialectically linked to emergent problems in capitalist authority,[14] those waves are not simply a straightforward reflection of those societal developmental problems, which are cumulative, whilst the control-waves come and go.

Further, the possible contribution of the controlological programme may be to unravel the following kind of paradox by totally denying the 'common-sense view' of events, and by liberating the analysis of (crime and) control from its interpretive tyranny. In this way, Hall *et al.* (1978, p. 186) attempt:

> to put the matter in the form of a paradox: it is important to reject the common-sense view that, when all is said and done, muggers mugged, the police picked them up, and the courts put them away, and that is that. But it is also important to insist that some muggers *did* mug, that 'mugging' *was* a real social and historical event arising out of its own kind of struggle, and that it has its own rational and historical 'logic' which we need to unravel.

It is slightly unfair to quote this (although I have not misquoted) since the rest of their book takes great care to illustrate the proposition that people did *not* 'do' muggings, and that, on the contrary, the *term* 'mugging' 'did for' several youths who would have received 6 months under earlier linguistic regimes, but who after 1970 received sentences of up to 20 years. To occasionally view 'muggings' as part of the repertoire of working-class action, rather than as exclusively part of the rhetoric of ruling-class control, is to sacrifice full understanding and complete autonomy from dominant theorising upon the altar of short-term understanding and acceptability. The point is: I am *not* being ironic. To lapse ultimately into common sense is to collapse into the most pernicious (because its class nature is concealed) form of ruling idea. Inevitably, it is common sense that criminals commit crimes rather than, as I have suggested, the courts. But because it is 'obvious', that doesn't make it worth believing. In fact one might even believe, with Laing (1968), that the obviousness or commonsensicality of a proposition is sufficient warrant for believing it to be analytic nonsense. Controlology, or final liberation from 'criminology', must include liberation from those lay opinions and attitudes (common sense) of which positivistic criminology is merely an intellectual extension and costly justification.

NOTES

1. This is not, on the other hand, to claim that situational ethnography isn't a form of control *itself* – at least when societal implications are drawn from situational work. Situational ethnography needs to be understood for what it *is* (the organisation of subjects' interpretations and accounts within a framework that makes them 'ordinary': Ditton, 1977, p. 11); and for what it clearly is *not*: a final and authenticated account of what is 'really' going on. In the earlier book (Ditton, 1977), a situational ethnography of similar activities in the same bakery, it made considerable sense to claim (as I did there) that the men were, on their *own* terms, 'fiddling', 'stealing' and 'dealing'. From a societal perspective, however, given that the main resource that the ethnographer has in interpreting meanings is talk, because of the ever present possibility of rationalisation and lying, my decision to present the account that a person was 'dealing' is a particular framing of talk, which may itself have also included the alternative account (which I didn't choose) that 'it was a mistake'. To use Goffman's (1974) model, the situational ethnographic account attempts to pierce the frame to its 'core' (to see what was 'really' initially *intended*); and the societal ethnographic account is more than satisfied with its 'rim' (to understand what 'really' then *happened*). Accordingly, Chapter 2's societal rendering of the events described situationally in Chapter 3 as 'dealing', is to portray them as 'acts' and not as 'crimes'. Neither Keith nor Doug was taken to court: neither has a 'criminal' record based upon the episodes discussed.

2. This is not the usual criticism-deflecting pre-emptive hedge, described by Scull (1977, p. 11) as 'the initial acknowledgement that those who label (or who construct or impose new labels) are more powerful than those who are labelled [which] represents a dismal substitute for the analysis of power structures and their impact'; nor is it an example of the regular unconventional sentimentality which portrays those labelled as the wretched victims of villainous control. A whole range of people, businessmen, the military, the police, doctors, husbands, and so on, *do acts* for example like killing other people (see note 17, Chapter 2) from which only a small number is selected for murder indictments. This has two implications: firstly (logically), only the latter sample are 'murderers' (it's the intent, and not the effect that counts); but secondly, since guilty verdicts can be produced even when the eventual offender denies initial intent, and also may *not* emerge (through the application of defeats like accident, coercion, duress, provocation, insanity or infancy) even when that initial intent has been admitted, then it is not even the intent that counts – merely the verdict; and that verdict is produced, in the last instance, wholly by control. Consequently, criminal statistics can only give a collation of an extremely biased sample of (in this case) deaths. Now, if the intent is to study criminal statistics as topic – the typically spurned ethnomethodological programme – this would not be a

difficulty. But it is precisely because those statistics are generally and uncritically treated as resource, that the basis of their collection should be expanded to include *all* sociologically similar (items, again, in this case) deaths, and their collation should be on the logical basis of their *effect*, rather than, as now, on the irrelevant basis of their retrospectively created intent.

3. Both the form and the substance of these activities are 'fungible': that is, both legitimate issuing and illegitimate 'dealing', and legitimate and stolen bread are indistinguishable from each other – *behaviourally*.

4. Often collected at workplaces as folk memories (see, particularly, Horning, 1963, p. 150–9), and sometimes analysed by sociologists as displaying, by example, normatively tolerated pilferage levels. It might be more appropriate to view the function of such episodes as horror-stories regaling what can happen, rather than as warning-tales, relating what may be done.

5. This attitude, which I have termed 'Controlology', should be distinguished from 'control theory' [see Hirschi (1969) and Box (1971)]. The research implication of control theory – rarely implemented – is not to ask 'Why do they do it?', but rather 'Why don't we do it?' This is treated as a wholly positivist recasting of labelling, and not (as with controlology) as a wholly *anti*-positivist recasting of labelling.

6. Fig. 4.1 may fruitfully be compared with Figs. 2.6 and 3.3. Of the two conceivable methods of establishing whether or not control can be said to 'work' (the consequential-pragmatic: simply whether or not the result is less crime; or the intentional-analytic: whether or not the result, in terms of an initial situation, matches the conventionally supposed inverse relationship between crime and control), I have consistently chosen the former.

7. See Ross, Campbell and Glass (1970) or Ball *et al.* (1978).

8. See Baldwin and Bottoms (1976).

9. See J. Young (1971) or S. Cohen (1973).

10. See Kutchinsky (1973) or Mathiesen (1974).

11. Controlology is not an institutional claim for a new discipline; it is only a plea that control might be considered an authentically separable topic for study, which, in the light of the discussion of the institutional failings of traditional labelling and Marxist theorists given in Chapter 1, is organised as a replacement for and not just a rejection of criminology. It would obviously be overwhelmingly pretentious to make broad policy recommendations, since I am only really concerned with establishing a preliminary logical and analytic warrant for the separate study of control. Nevertheless it is clear that controlology directly opposes criminology (which grew up arm-in-arm with social control, and is organised to study the conditions of the criminal impulse) in that it could well be used as an arm against social control, through its study of the control impulse. The political relationship to labelling is more difficult to establish. Ericson (1975, p. 121) suggests that the reason why labellers have failed to produce valid policy recommendations are precisely those analytic gaps that controlology fills:

> Labelling analysts have been slow to link their theory and research to its implications for criminal law and punishment. This is related to the fact that the premises of the labelling perspective itself have not always been adequately clarified.

Edwin Schur has taken it upon himself to spell out the obvious policy implications of labelling: and when so spelled, they appear particularly daft and passive. He says (1973, pp. 154–5):

> Basically, radical nonintervention implies policies that accommodate society to the widest possible diversity of behaviours and attitudes, rather than forcing as many individuals as possible to 'adjust' to supposedly common societal standards. . . . Thus, the basic injunction for public policy becomes: *leave kids alone wherever possible.*

It is at least possible, then, that a full working out of the premises of the labelling perspective could sponsor weightier policy recommendations.

12. Which Lemert, in the 1972 Introduction to Lemert, 1967 (quoted in Scull, 1977, p. 11), refers to as '*reductio ad personam* theory'.

13. Apart from the logical failings (which I pointed out in Chapter 2), these were chiefly a sort of bland ahistorical pluralism, available, in such asides as (Cohen, 1973, p. 28) 'Societies appear to be subject, every now and then, to periods of moral panic'.

14. There is no (nor could there be any) explanation in Hall *et al.* of why the mugging crime wave eventually collapsed as it did.

Bibliography

Akers, Ronald L. (1967–8), 'Problems in the Sociology of Deviance: Social Definitions and Behaviour', *Social Forces*, **46**, pp. 455–65.

Anon. (1863), 'The Science of Garotting and Housebreaking', *Cornhill Magazine*, **VII**, Jan., pp. 79–92.

Armstrong, Gail, and Wilson, Mary (1973), 'City Politics and Deviancy Amplification', pp. 61–89 in Taylor, I. and Taylor, L. (eds.), 1973.

Atkinson, J. Maxwell (1971), 'Societal Reactions to Suicide: The Role of Coroners' Definitions', in S. Cohen (ed.), 1971, pp. 165–91.

Atkinson, J. Maxwell (1974), 'Versions of Deviance', *Soc. Rev.*, **22**, no. 4, Nov., pp. 616–25.

Atkinson, J. Maxwell (1978), *Discovering Suicide: Studies in the Social Organisation of Sudden Death* (London: Macmillan).

Bailey, Roy and Brake, Mike (eds.) (1975), *Radical Social Work* (London: Edward Arnold).

Baker, George W. and Chapman, Dwight W. (eds.) (1962), *Man and Society in Disaster* (New York: Basic Books).

Baldwin, John and Bottoms, A. E. (1976), *The Urban Criminal: A Study in Sheffield* (London: Tavistock).

Balk, Alfred (1962), 'Confessions of a Block-Buster', *Saturday Evening Post* (reprint), **235**, no. 27, 14, 21 July, pp. 15–19.

Ball, John, Chester, Lewis and Perrott, Roy (1978), *Cops and Robbers: An Investigation into Armed Bank Robbery* (London: André Deutsch).

Ball, Richard A. (1966), 'An Empirical Exploration of Neutralisation Theory', *Criminologica*, **4**, Aug., pp. 255–65.

Bankowski, Zenon, Mungham, Geoff and Young, Peter (1977), 'Radical Criminology or Radical Criminologist?', *Contemp. Crisis*, **1**, pp. 37–52.

Beattie, J. M. (1972), 'Toward a Study of Crime in 18th Century England: A Note on Indictments', in P. Fritz and D. Williams (eds.), pp. 299–314.

Beattie, J. M. (1974), 'The Pattern of Crime in England 1660–1800', *P. and P.*, **62**, pp. 47–95.

Beattie, R. H. (1955), 'Problems of Criminal Statistics in the United States', *J.C.L., C., & P.S.*, **46**, pp. 178–86.

Beattie, R. H. (1960), 'Criminal Statistics in the United States – 1960', *J.C.L., C., & P.S.*, **51**, pp. 49–65.

Becker, Howard S. (1960), 'Notes on the Concept of Commitment', *A. J. S.*, **66**, July, pp. 32–40. In Howard S. Becker (ed.) 1970.

Becker, Howard S. (1963), *Outsiders* (New York: Free Press).

Becker, Howard S. (ed.) (1964), *The Other Side* (New York: Free Press).

Becker, Howard S. (1967), 'Whose Side are we On?', *Soc. Probs.*, **14**, (Winter), pp. 239–47, and in Becker (ed.) 1970.

Becker, Howard S. (ed.) (1970), *Sociological Work: Method and Substance* (London: Allen Lane).

Becker, Howard S. (1970a), Dialogue, in *Issues in Crim.*, **5**, no. 2 (Summer), pp. 159–79.

Becker, Howard S. (1973), 'Labelling Theory Reconsidered', in Rock and McIntosh (eds.) 1974, pp. 41–66. [From Becker 1963, revised edn.]

Bell, Daniel (1960), *The End of Ideology* (New York: Free Press).

Bell, Daniel (1960a), 'The Myth of Crime Waves', in Bell, 1960, pp. 151–74.

Beyleveld, Deryck and Wiles, Paul (1975), 'Man and Method in David Matza's "Becoming Deviant"', *B. J. Crim.*, **15**, no. 2, Apr., pp. 111–27.

Biderman, Albert D. and Reiss, Albert J. (1967), 'On Exploring the "Dark Figure" of Crime', *Annals A.A.P.S.S.*, **374**, Nov., pp. 1–15.

Black, Donald J. (1970), 'Production of Crime Rates', *A.S.R.*, **35**, Aug., pp. 733–48.

Bordua, David J. (1967) (ed.), *The Police: Six Sociological Essays* (New York: J. Wiley and Sons).

Bottomley, A. Keith and Coleman, Clive A. (1976), 'Criminal Statistics: The Police Role in the Discovery and Detection of Crime', *I.J.C.P.*, **4**, pp. 33–58.

Box, Stephen (1971), *Deviance, Reality and Society* (London: Holt, Rinehart & Winston).

Brennan, William C. (1974), 'Abortion and the Techniques of Neutralisation', *J. of H. & S.B.*, **15**, no. 4, pp. 358–65.

Broadhead, Robert S. (1974), 'A Theoretical Critique of the Societal Reaction Approach to Deviance', *Pacific S.R.*, **17**, no. 3, July, pp. 287–312.

Bucher, R. (1957), 'Blame and Hostility in Disaster', *A.J.S.*, **6**, Mar., pp. 467–75.

Buckner, H. Taylor (1968), 'The Flying Saucerians: An Open Door Cult', in M. Truzzi (ed.), 1968, pp. 223–30.

Bunyan, Tony (1976), *The Political Police in Britain* (London: Julian Friedmann Publishers).

Campbell, Donald T. and Ross, H. Lawrence (1968), 'The Connecticut Crackdown on Speeding: Time-Series Data in Quasi-Experimental Analysis', *Law and Soc. Rev.*, **3**, no. 1, pp. 33–53.

Cantril, Hadley (1952), 'The Invasion From Mars', in Swanson, Newcomb and Hartley (eds.), 1952, pp. 198–207.

Carson, W. G. and Wiles, Paul (eds.) (1970), *Crime and Delinquency in Britain* (London: M. Robertson).

Carson, W. G. (1970), 'Some Sociological Aspects of Strict Liability and the Enforcement of Factory Legislation', *Mod. L. Rev.*, **33**, July, pp. 396–412.

Center, Lawrence J. and Smith Thomas G. (1973), 'Criminal Statistics – Can they be Trusted?', *Am. Crim. Law Rev.*, **11**, no. 4 (Summer), pp. 1045–86.

Chambliss, William J. (1964), 'A Sociological Analysis of the Law and Vagrancy', *Soc. Probs.*, **12** (Summer), pp. 67–77. In Carson and Wiles (eds.), 1971, pp. 206–19.

Chambliss, William J. (1971), 'Vice, Corruption, Bureaucracy, and Power', *Wisconsin L.R.*, no. 4, pp. 1150–73.

Chambliss, William J. (1975), 'The Political Economy of Crime: A Comparative Study of Nigeria and the USA', in Taylor, Walton and Young (eds.), 1975, pp. 167–80.

Chambliss, William J. (1975a), 'Toward a Political Economy of Crime', *Theory and Society*, **2** (Summer), pp. 149–70.

Chapman, Dwight W. (1962), 'A Brief Introduction to Contemporary Disaster Research', in Baker and Chapman (eds.), 1962, pp. 3–22.

Cicourel, Aaron V. (1968), *The Social Organisation of Juvenile Justice* (London: H.E.B.).

Clay, John (1855), 'On the Effect of Good or Bad Times on Committals to Prison', *J.S.S.L.*, **18**, Mar., pp. 74–9.

Cohen, Morris R. (1931), 'Fictions', pp. 226–8 *Encly. of Soc. Sci.*, **III**, and in R. Dubin (ed.), 1968, pp. 489–93.

Cohen, Stanley (ed.) (1971), *Images of Deviance* (Harmondsworth: Penguin).

Cohen, Stanley (1973), *Folk Devils and Moral Panics* (London: Paladin).

Cohen, Stanley (1974), 'Criminology and the Sociology of Deviance in Britain: A Recent History and a Current Report', in Rock and McIntosh (eds.), 1974, pp. 1–40.

Cohen, Stanley (1975), 'It's Alright For You to Talk: Political and Sociological Manifestos for Social Work Action', pp. 76–95 in Bailey and Brake (eds.), 1975.

C.O.I. (Reference Division) (1973), *The Prevention and Treatment of Drug Dependence in Britain* (Pamphlet, H.M.S.O.).

Coleman, Clive A. and Bottomley, A. Keith (1976), 'Police Conceptions of Crime and "No Crime"', *Crim. L. Rev.*, June, pp. 344–60.

Conklin, J. E. (1975), *The Impact of Crime* (New York: Macmillan).

Cooley, Charles Horton (1902), *Human Nature and the Social Order* (New York: Schocken Books).

Cooper, David (ed.) (1968), *The Dialectics of Liberation* (Harmondsworth: Penguin).

Coulter, Jeff (1974), 'What's Wrong with the New Criminology?', *Soc. Rev.*, **22**, no. 1, pp. 119–35.

Damer, Sean (1974), 'Wine Alley: The Sociology of a Dreadful Enclosure', *Soc. Rev.*, **22**, no. 2, May, pp. 175–206.

Davis, Fred (1961), 'Deviance Disavowal: The Management of Strained Interaction by the Visibly Handicapped', *Soc. Probs.*, **9**, pp. 120–32, and in Filstead (ed), 1972.

Davis, Fred and Olesen, Virginia (1970), 'Initiation into a Woman's Profession: Identity Problems in the Status Transition of Coed to Student Nurse', *Sociometry*, **3**, pp. 89–107.

Davis, Nanette J. (1972), 'Labelling Theory in Deviance Research: A Critique and Reconsideration', *Soc. Quart.*, **13** (Fall), pp. 447–74.

Dickson, Donald T. (1968–9), 'Bureaucracy and Morality: An Organisational Perspective on a Moral Crusade', *Soc. Probs.*, **16**, pp. 143–57.

Ditton, Jason (1972), 'The Problem of Time: Styles of Time-Management and Schemes of Time-Manipulation Amongst Machine-Paced Workers', *Working Paper no. 2* (Durham University).

Ditton, Jason (1972a), 'Absent at Work: Or How to Manage Monotony', *New Soc.*, 21.12.72, pp. 679–81.

Ditton, Jason (1976), 'Baking Time', Paper to B.S.A. Annual Conf., 7.4.76, *Mimeo.* [*Soc. Rev.* (forthcoming) 1979].

Ditton, Jason (1977), *Part-Time Crime: An Ethnography of Fiddling and Pilferage* (London: Macmillan).

Ditton, Jason (forthcoming) (1980), *Insiders: A Sociological Theory of Part-Time Theft* (London: Macmillan).

Doleschal, Eugene, and Klapmuts, Nora (1973), 'Toward a New Criminology', *C. and D. Lit.*, **5**, no. 4, Dec., pp. 607–26; and in Radzinowicz and Wolfgang (1977) (eds.), **1**, Ch. 34, pp. 639–57.

Douglas, Jack D. (ed.) (1970), *Deviance and Respectability* (New York: Basic Books).

Douglas, Jack D. (ed.) (1970a), *Observations of Deviance* (New York: Random House).

Douglas, Jack D. (1971), *American Social Order: Social Rules in a Pluralistic Society* (New York: Free Press).

Drabeck, Thomas E. and Quarantelli, Enrico L. (1967), 'Scapegoats, Villains and Disasters', *Transaction*, **4**, no. 4, Mar., pp. 12–18. In James F. Short (ed.), 1970, pp. 161–75.

Dubin, R. (ed.) (1968), *Human Relations in Administration* (New Jersey: Prentice-Hall).

Du Cane, E. F. (1893), 'The Decrease in Crime', *The Nineteenth Century*, **33**, Mar., pp. 480–92.

Emerson, Tony (1975), *Mass Communication – or Mass Deception* (London: Key Issue Publications).

Engels, Frederick (1845), *The Condition of the Working Class in England* (Moscow: Progress).

Ericson, Richard V. (1975), *Criminal Reactions: The Labelling Perspective* (Farnborough: Saxon House).

Erikson, Kai T. (1962), 'Notes on the Sociology of Deviance', *Soc. Probs.*, **9** (Fall), pp. 307–14, and in Becker (ed.), 1964, pp. 9–24.

Erikson, Kai T. (1966), *Wayward Puritans: A Study in the Sociology of Deviance* (New York: J. Wiley and Sons).

Ferracuti, Franco, Hernandez, Rosita P. and Wolfgang, Marvin E. (1962), 'A Study of Police Errors in Crime Classification', *J.C.L., C., & P.S.*, **53**, pp. 113–19.

Filstead, William J. (ed.) (1972), *An Introduction to Deviance* (New York: Markham).

Fine, Bob (1977), 'Labelling Theory: An Investigation into the Sociological Critique of Deviance', *Econ. and Soc.*, **6**, no. 2, May, pp. 166–93.

Fletcher, Joseph (1849), 'Moral and Educational Statistics of England and Wales', *J.S.S.L.*, **12**, pp. 151–349.

Fordham, Peta (1965), *The Robber's Tale: The Real Story of the Great Train Robbery* (Harmondsworth: Penguin).

Friedrichs, Robert W. (1970), *A Sociology of Sociology* (London: Collier-Macmillan).

Fritz, Charles E. (1961), 'Disaster', in Merton and Nisbet (eds.) (1st edn.) pp. 651–94.

Fritz, P. and Williams, D. (eds.) (1972), *The Triumph of Culture* (Toronto: Hakkert).

Bibliography   113

Gatrell, V. A. C. and Hadden, T. B. (1972), 'Criminal Statistics and their Interpretation', in Wrigley (ed.), 1972, pp. 336–96.

Gibbons, Don C. and Rooney, Elizabeth A. (1966), 'Social Reactions to "Crimes without Victims"', *Soc. Probs.*, Spring, **13**, pp. 400–10.

Gibbons, Don C. and Jones, Joseph F. (1971), 'Some Critical Notes on Current Definitions of Deviance', *Pacific S.R.*, **14**, pp. 20–37.

Gibbs, Jack P. (1966), 'Conceptions of Deviant Behaviour: The Old and the New', *Pacific.S.R.*, **9**, no. 2, Spring, pp. 9–14, and in Filstead (ed.), 1972.

Gill, Owen (1976), 'Urban Stereotypes and Delinquent Incidents', *B.J.Crim.*, **16**, no. 4, Oct., pp. 321–36.

Gillis, John R. (1975), 'The Evolution of Juvenile Delinquency in England, 1890–1914', *P. and P.*, no. 67, May, pp. 96–126.

Glasgow University Media Group (1976), *Bad News*, **1** (London: R.K.P.).

Glass, Gene V. (1968), 'Analysis of Data on the Connecticut Speeding Crackdown as a Time-Series Quasi-Experiment', *Law and Soc. Rev.*, **3**, no. 1, pp. 55–76.

Goffman, Erving (1963), *Stigma: Notes on the Management of Spoiled Identity* (Harmondsworth: Penguin).

Goffman, Erving (1974), *Frame Analysis: An Essay on the Organisation of Experience* (London: Peregrine).

Goode, Erich (1975), 'On Behalf of Labeling Theory', *Soc. Probs.*, **22**, no. 5, June, pp. 570–83.

Gordon, David M. (1971), 'Class and the Economics of Crime', *Rev. Rad. Pol. Econ.*, **3**, 5, pp. 51–75.

Gordon, David M. (1973), 'Capitalism, Class and Crime in America', *Crime and Del.*, **19**, Apr., pp. 163–86.

Gouldner, Alvin W. (1968), 'The Sociologist as Partisan: Sociology and the Welfare State', *Am. Soc.*, May, **3**, no. 2, pp. 103–16.

Gove, Walter R. (1970), 'Societal Reaction as an Explanation of Mental Illness: An Evaluation', *A.S.R.*, Oct., **35**, pp. 873–84.

Hagan, John (1972), 'Labelling and Deviance: A Case Study in the "Sociology of the Interesting"', *Soc. Probs.*, **20**, no. 4, pp. 447–58.

Hall, Stuart, Critcher, Chas., Jefferson, Tony, Clarke, John, Roberts, Brian (1978), *Policing the Crisis: Mugging, the State, and Law and Order* (London: Macmillan).

Hanawalt, Barbara (1974), 'Economic Influences on the Pattern of Crime in England, 1300–1348', *Am. J. of L. Hist.*, **XIX**, Oct., pp. 281–97.

Hay, Douglas, Linebaugh, Peter, Rule, John G., Thompson, E. P. and Winslow, Cal. (eds.) (1975), *Albion's Fatal Tree: Crime and Society in Eighteenth Century England* (London: Allen Lane).

Hepworth, Mike, and Turner, Bryan S. (1974), 'Confessing to Murder: Critical Notes on the Sociology of Motivation', *B.J.L.S.*, **1**, no. 1, pp. 31–49.

Hindess, Barry (1973), *The Use of Official Statistics in Sociology: A Critique of Positivism and Ethnomethodology* (London: Macmillan).

Hirschi, Travis (1969), *Causes of Delinquency* (Berkeley: Univ. California Press).

Hirschi, Travis (1973), 'Procedural Rules and the Study of Deviant Behaviour', *Soc. Probs.*, **21**, no. 2, pp. 159–73.

Hirst, Paul Q. (1975), 'Marx and Engels on Law, Crime and Morality', in Taylor, Walton and Young (eds.), 1975, Ch. 8, pp. 203–32.

Hobbs, Albert H. (1943), 'Relationship between Criminality and Economic

Conditions', *J.C.L., C., & P.S.*, **34**, May/June, pp. 5–10.

Hood, Roger and Sparks, Richard (1970), *Key Issues in Criminology* (London: Weidenfeld and Nicolson (W.U.L.)).

Horning, Donald M. (1963), 'Blue-Collar Theft: A Study of Pilfering by Industrial Workers' (*Unpub.*, Ph.D.), (Indiana University).

Hughes, Everett C. (1951), 'Mistakes at Work', *The Canadian J. of Econ. and Pol. Sci.*, **XVII**, Aug., pp. 320–7. Ch. 7 in Hughes, 1958.

Hughes, Everett C. (1958), *Men and their Work* (London: Free Press).

Hughes, Patrick H., Barker, Noel W., Crawford, Gail A. and Jaffe, Jerome H. (1972), 'The Natural History of a Heroin Epidemic', *J. Am. Pub. Health Assn.*, **62**, no. 7, July, pp. 995–1001.

Hunt, Leon Gibson and Chambers, Carl D. (1976), *The Heroin Epidemics: A Study of Heroin Use in the United States, 1965–1975* (London: Spectrum Publications).

Jacobs, Norman (1964), 'The Phantom Slasher of Taipei: Mass Hysteria in a Non-Western Society', *Soc. Probs.*, **12**, pp. 318–28.

Johnson, Donald M. (1945), 'The "Phantom Anesthetist" of Mattoon: A Field Study of Mass Hysteria', *J. Abnorm. Soc. Psy.*, **XL**, Apr., pp. 175–86.

Katz, Jack (1972–3), 'Deviance, Charisma, and Rule-Defined Behaviour', *Soc. probs.*, **20**, no. 2, pp. 186–202.

Katz, Jack (1975), 'Essences as Moral Identities: Verifiability and Responsibility in Imputations of Deviance and Charisma', *A.J.S.*, **80**, no. 6, May, pp. 1369–90.

Kitsuse, John I. and Dietrick, D. C. (1959), 'Delinquent Boys: A Critique', *A.S.R.*, **24**, no. 2, pp. 213–15.

Kitsuse, John I. (1962), 'Societal Reactions to Deviant Behaviour', *Soc. Probs.*, **9**, no. 2, and in Becker (ed.), 1964, pp. 87–102.

Kitsuse, John I. and Cicourel, Aaron V, (1963), 'A Note on the Uses of Official Statistics', *Soc. Probs.*, **12**, pp. 131–9. Also in Filstead (ed.), 1972, pp. 244–55.

Kitsuse, John I. (1972), 'Deviance, Deviant Behaviour, and Deviants: Some Conceptual Problems', in Filstead (ed.), 1972, pp. 233–43.

Klapp, Orrin E. (1956), 'American Villain Types', *A.S.R.*, **21**, June, pp. 337–40.

Klapp, Orrin E. (1959), 'Notes Towards the Study of Vilification as a Social Process', *Pacific S.R.*, **2**, (Fall), pp. 71–6.

Knutsson, Johannes (1977), *Labelling Theory: A Critical Examination*, SRG Report no. 3, Stockholm.

Kuhn, Thomas S. (1970), *The Structure of Scientific Revolutions*, (2nd edn.) (Chicago: Univ. of Chicago Press).

Kutchinsky, Berl. (1973), 'Eroticism without Censorship: Sociological Investigations on the Production and Consumption of Pornographic Literature in Denmark', *I.J.C.P.*, **1**, pp. 217–25.

Laing, R. D., Phillipson, H. and Lee, A. R. (1966), *Interpersonal Perception* (London: Tavistock).

Laing, R. D. (1968), 'The Obvious', pp. 13–33 in D. Cooper (ed.), 1968.

Lakatos, I. and Musgrave (eds.) (1970), *Criticism and the Growth of Knowledge* (Cambridge: C.U.P.).

Larner, Christina (1977), 'The Crime of Witchcraft in Scotland', *Mimeo* (University of Glasgow).

Lemert, Edwin M. (1951), *Social Pathology* (New York: McGraw-Hill).

Lemert, Edwin M. (1967), *Human Deviance, Social Problems, and Social Control* (New Jersey: Prentice-Hall).

Lemert, Edwin M. (1970), *Social Action and Legal Change* (Chicago: Aldine).

Lemert, Edwin M. (1974), 'Beyond Mead: The Societal Reaction to Deviance', *Soc. Probs.*, **21**, no. 4, pp. 457–68.

Levin, Yale and Lindesmith, Alfred (1937), 'English Ecology and Criminology of the Past Century', *J.C.L. & C.*, **27**, Mar/Apr., pp. 801–16.

Levine, James P. (1976), 'The Potential for Crime Overreporting in Criminal Victimisation Surveys', *Criminology*, **14**, no. 4, Nov., pp. 307–30.

Levitin, Teresa E. (1975), 'Deviants as Active Participants in the Labeling Process: the Visibly Handicapped', *Soc. Probs.*, **22**, no. 4, pp. 548–57.

Liazos, Alexander (1972), 'The Poverty of the Sociology of Deviance: Nuts, Sluts, and Perverts', *Soc. Probs.*, **20**, no. 1, pp. 103–20.

Lindesmith, A. R. (1965), *The Addict and the Law* (New York: Vintage Books).

Linebaugh, Peter (1975), 'Tyburn: A Study of Crime and the Labouring Poor in London During the First Half of the Eighteenth Century', Centre for the Study of social History (*Unpub.* Ph.D.), (Warwick University).

Lofland, John (1969), *Deviance and Identity* (New York: Prentice-Hall).

McClintock, F. M. (1970), 'The Dark Figure', in vol. 5 of the *Collected Studies in Criminological Research*, pp. 9–34 (Council of Europe).

McIntosh, Mary (1971), 'Changes in the Organisation of Thieving', in Stanley Cohen (ed.), 1971.

Mackay, Charles (1852), *Extraordinary Popular Delusions and the Madness of Crowds* (London: Allen and Unwin).

Mankoff, Milton (1971), 'Societal Reaction and Career Deviance: A Critical Analysis', *Soc. Quart.*, **12** (Spring), pp. 204–18.

Mannheim, Herman (1965), *Comparative Criminology: A Text Book* (2 vols.) (London: R.K.P.).

Manning, Peter K. (1975), 'Deviance and Dogma: Some Comments on the Labeling Perspective', *B. J. Crim.*, **15**, no. 1, Jan., pp. 1–20.

Manning, Peter K. (1977), *Police Work: The Social Organisation of Policing* (London: M.I.T. Press).

Maruyama, Margoroh (1960), 'Morphogenesis and Morphostasis', *Methodos*, **XII**, 48, pp. 251–96.

Maruyama, Margoroh (1963), 'The Second Cybernetics: Deviation-Amplifying Mutual Causal Processes', *Am. Sci.*, **51**, pp. 164–79.

Masterman, M. (1970), 'The Nature of a Paradigm', in Lakatos and Musgrave (eds.), 1970.

Mathiesen, Thomas (1974), *The Politics of Abolition: Essays in Political Action Theory*, Scandinavian Studies in Criminology, **4**, (London: Robertson).

Matza, David (1964), *Delinquency and Drift* (New York: J. Wiley and Sons).

Matza, David (1969), *Becoming Deviant* (New Jersey: Prentice-Hall).

Mayhew, Henry (1862), *London Labour and the London Poor: A Cyclopedia of the Conditions and Earnings of Those that Will Work, Those that Cannot Work, and Those that Will Not Work* (London: Griffin, Bohn and Co.).

Mayhew, Henry and Binny, John (1862), *The Criminal Prisons of London and Scenes of Prison Life* (London: Frank Cass and Co.).

Medalia, Nahum Z. and Larsen, Otto N. (1958), 'Diffusion and Belief in a Collective Delusion: The Seattle Windshield Pitting Epidemic', *A.S.R.*, **23**, pp. 180–9.

Megaree, Edwin I. (1977), 'Crime and Delinquency', in Sagarin and Montanino (eds.), 1977, pp. 18–87.

Merton, Robert K. (1968), *Social Theory and Social Structure* (New York: Free Press).

Merton, Robert A. and Nisbet, Robert A. (eds.) (1966), *Contemporary Social Problems*, 2nd edn. (New York: Harcourt Brace).

Mitchell, Wesley Clair (1941), *Business Cycles and Their Causes* (Berkeley: Univ. of California Press).

Monkkonen, Eric H. (1976), *The Dangerous Class: Crime and Poverty in Columbus, Ohio, 1860–1885* (London: Harvard Univ. Press).

Morrison, William Douglas (1892), 'The Increase of Crime', *The Nineteenth Century*, **31**, no. 84, June, pp. 950–7.

Morrison, William Douglas (1897), 'The Interpretation of Criminal Statistics', *J. Royal Stat. Soc.*, **LX**, Mar. (1), pp. 1–24.

Mugford, Stephen K. (1974), 'Marxism and Criminology: A Comment on the Symposium Review on "The New Criminology" ', *Soc. Quart.*, **15** (Autumn), pp. 591–6.

Nettler, Gwynn (1974), 'Embezzlement without Problems', *B.J. Crim.*, **14**, no. 1, Jan., pp. 70–7.

Newman, Graeme R. (1973), 'A Theory of Deviance Removal', *B.J.S.*, **XXVI**, 2, pp. 203–17.

Noble, J. V. (1977), 'Feedback Instability and Crime Waves', *J.R.C.D.*, **14**, no. 1, Jan., pp. 107–28.

N.P.D.S. (Northumbria Police Drug Squad) (1976), 'Drug Abuse and Addiction' (*Mimeo*, Northumbria Police).

Pearce, Frank (1976), *Crimes of the Powerful: Marxism, Crime and Deviance* (London: Pluto Press).

Pearson, Geoffrey (1975), *The Deviant Imagination* (London: Macmillan).

Phelps, Harold A. (1929), 'Cycles of Crime', *J.C.L., C., & P.S.*, **20**, May/June, pp. 107–21.

Philips, David (1977), *Crime and Authority in Victorian England: The Black Country, 1835–1860* (London: Croom Helm).

Pine, Vanderlyn R. (1974), 'Grief Work and Dirty Work: The Aftermath of an Aircrash', *Omega*, **5**, no. 4, pp. 281–6.

Plummer, Ken (1978), 'Misunderstanding Labelling Perspectives', forthcoming in D. Downes and P. Rock (eds.) *Deviant Interpretations* (London: M. Robertson).

Potter, Ellen C. (1926), 'Spectacular Aspects of Crime in Relation to the Crime Wave', *Annals A.A.P.S.S.*, 125, May, pp. 1–19.

Priest, Thomas Brian and McGrath, John H. III (1970), 'Techniques of Neutralisation: Young Adult Marihuana Smokers', *Criminologica*, Aug., **8**, pp. 185–94.

Quarantelli, E. L. (1955), 'The Nature and Conditions of Panic', *A.J.S.*, **60**, pp. 267–75.

Quinney, Richard (1970), *The Social Reality of Crime* (Boston: Little, Brown and Co.).

Quinney, Richard (1975), 'What do Crime Rates Mean?', in Radzinowicz and Wolfgang (eds.), 2nd edn., **1**, 1977, pp. 107–11.

Radzinowicz, L. (1941), 'The Influence of Economic Conditions on Crime – I', *Soc. Rev.*, **33**, no. 2, Jan/Apr., pp. 1–36.

Radzinowicz, L. (1941a), 'The Influence of Economic Conditions on Crime – II', *Soc. Rev.*, **33**, no. 3, 1941, pp. 139–53.

Radzinowicz, Sir Leon and Wolfgang, Marvin E. (eds.) (1977), *Crime and Justice*, 2nd & Revised edn: vol. I, *The Criminal in Society*; vol. II, *The Criminal in the Arms of the Law*; vol. III, *The Criminal Under Restraint* (New York: Basic Books).

Rau, Nicholas (1974), *Trade Cycles: Theory and Evidence* (London: Macmillan).

Rawson, Rawson W. (1839), 'An Inquiry into the Statistics of Crime in England and Wales', *J. Stat. Soc.*, **2**, Oct., pp. 316–44.

Robertson, Roland and Taylor, Laurie (1973), *Deviance, Crime and Socio-Legal Control: Comparative Perspectives* (London: M. Robertson).

Robertson, Roland and Taylor, Laurie (1974), 'Problems in the Comparative Analysis of Deviance', in Rock and McIntosh (eds.), 1974, pp. 91–123.

Rock, Paul (1973), 'Phenomenalism and Essentialism in the Sociology of Deviance', *Sociology*, **7**, no. 1, pp. 18–29.

Rock, Paul (1973a), *Deviant Behaviour* (London: Hutchinson).

Rock, Paul (1973b), Review of The New Criminology, *Soc. Quant.*, **14**, Aug., pp. 594–5.

Rock, Paul and McIntosh (eds.) (1974), *Deviance and Social Control* (London: Tavistock).

Rock, Paul (1974), 'The Sociology of Deviance and Conceptions of the Moral Order', *B.J. Crim.*, **14**, no. 2, pp. 139–49.

Rock, Paul (1977), 'The Sociology of Crime, Symbolic Interactionism and some Problematic Qualities of Radical Criminology' (*Mimeo*, L.S.E.; paper given to Cambridge Criminology Conf. 3–5 July).

Rodgers, Joseph W. and Buffalo, M. D. (1974), 'Neutralisation Techniques: Toward a Simplified Measurement Scale', *Pacific S.R.*, **17**, no. 3, July, pp. 313–31.

Rodgers, Joseph W. and Buffalo, M. D. (1974a), 'Fighting Back: Nine Modes of Adaptation to a Deviant Label', *Soc. Probs.*, **22**, no. 1, Oct., pp. 101–18.

Roshier, Bob (1977), 'The Functions of Crime Myth', *Sociological Review*, **25**, no. 2, May, pp. 309–23.

Ross, H. Lawrence, Campbell, Donald T. and Glass, Gene V. (1970), 'Determining the Social Effects of Legal Reform: The British "Breathalyser" Crackdown of 1967', *Am. Behav. Sci.*, pp. 493–509.

Rotenberg, Mordechai (1974), 'Self-Labelling: A Missing Link in the "Societal Reaction" Theory of Deviance', *Soc. Rev.*, **22**, no. 3, pp. 335–54.

Rotenberg, Mordechai (1975), 'Self-Labelling Theory: Preliminary Findings Among Mental Patients', *B.J. Crim.*, **15**, no. 4, Oct., pp. 360–75.

Rubington, Earl and Weinberg, Martin S. (eds.) (1968), *Deviance: The Interactionist Perspective* (London: Macmillan).

Sagarin, Edward and Montanino, Fred (eds.) (1977), *Deviants: Voluntary Actors in a Hostile World* (New York: General Leaning Press).

Samaha, Joel (1974), *Law and Order in Historical Perspective* (London: Academic Press).

Scheff, Thomas J. (1966), *Being Mentally Ill: A Sociological Theory* (Chicago: Aldine Pub. Co.).

Scheff, Thomas J. (1974), 'The Labelling Theory of Mental Illness', *A.S.R.*, **39**, June, pp. 444–52.

Schervish, Paul G. (1973), 'The Labeling Perspective: Its Bias and Potential in the Study of Political Deviance', *Am. Soc.*, **8**, May, pp. 47–57.

Schuler, Edgar A. and Parenton, Vernon J. (1943), 'A Recent Epidemic of Hysteria in a Louisiana High School', *J. Soc. Psy.*, **17**, pp. 221–35.

Schur, Edwin M. (1962), 'Drug Addiction Under British Policy', *Soc. Probs.*, **9** (Fall), and in Howard S. Becker (ed.) 1964, pp. 67–83.

Schur, Edwin M. (1965), *Crimes Without Victims* (New Jersey: Prentice-Hall).

Schur, Edwin M. (1969), *Our Criminal Society* (New Jersey: Prentice-Hall).

Schur, Edwin M. (1971), *Labeling Deviant Behaviour* (New York: Harper and Row).

Schur, Edwin M. (1973), *Radical Non Intervention: Rethinking the Delinquency Problem* (New Jersey: Prentice-Hall).

Scott, Robert A. and Douglas, Jack D. (eds.) (1972), *Theoretical Perspectives on Deviance* (New York: Basic Books).

Scull, Andrew (1972), 'Social Control and the Amplification of Deviance', in Scott & Douglas (eds.) (1972) Ch. 11, pp. 282–314.

Scull, Andrew T. (1977), *Decarceration: Community Treatment and the Deviant – A Radical View* (New Jersey: Prentice-Hall).

Seidman, David and Couzens, Michael (1974), 'Getting the Crime Rate Down: Political Pressure and Crime Reporting', *L. & S. Rev.*, **8** (Spring), pp. 457–93.

Sellin, Thorsten (1951), 'The Significance of Records of Crime', *Law Q. Rev.*, **67**, pp. 489–504, and in Wolfgang, Savitz and Johnston (eds.), 1962, pp. 59–68.

Short, James F. (ed.) (1970), *Modern Criminals* (Transaction Inc., Aldine). Crimes', *Wash. State Coll. Res. Stud.*, **20**, pp. 36–41.

Short, James F. (ed.) (1970), *Modern Criminals*, Transaction Inc., Aldine.

Silver, Allan (1967), 'The Demand for Order in Civil Society: A Review of Some Themes in the History of Urban Crime, Police, and Riot', in David J. Bordua (ed.), 1967, pp. 1–24.

Skolnick, Jerome (1966), *Justice Without Trial* (New York: J. Wiley).

Sparks, Richard F., Genn, Hazel G. and Dodd, David J. (1977), *Surveying Victims: A Study of the Measurement of Criminal Victimisation, Perceptions of Crime, and Attitudes to Criminal Justice* (London: J. Wiley).

Spitzer, Steven (1975), 'Towards a Marxian Theory of Deviance', *Soc. Probs.*, **22**, no. 5, June, pp. 638–51.

Steadman-Jones, Gareth (1977), 'Class Expression versus Social Control? A Critique of Recent Trends in the Social History of "Leisure"', *Hist. W. J.*, no. 4, Aug., pp. 162–70.

Sudnow, David (1964), 'Normal Crimes: Sociological Features of the Penal Code in a Public Defender Court', *Soc. Probs.*, **12**, no. 3, pp. 255–76.

Sumner, Colin (1977), 'Marxism and Deviancy Theory', in Wiles (ed.), 1977, pp. 159–74.

Swanson, Guy E., Newcomb, T. M. and Hartley, Eugene H. (eds.) (1952), *Readings in Social Psychology* (New York: Holt).

Sykes, Gresham M. (1974), 'The Rise of Critical Criminology', *J.C.L. & C.*, **65**, no. 2, June, pp. 206–13.

Talese, Gay (1971), *Honor Thy Father* (New York: Souvenir Press).

Taylor, Ian and Taylor, Laurie (eds.) (1973), *Politics and Deviance*, (Harmondsworth: Penguin).

Taylor, Ian, Walton, Paul and Young, Jock (1973), *The New Criminology* (London: R.K.P.).

Taylor, Ian, Walton, Paul and Young, Jock (eds.) (1975), *Critical Criminology* (London: R.K.P.).

Taylor, Laurie (1971), *Deviance and Society* (New York: Michael Joseph).

Thio, Alex (1973), 'Class Bias in the Sociology of Deviance', *Am. Soc.*, **18**, pp. 1–12.

Thomas, Dorothy Swaine (1927), *Social Aspects of the Business Cycle*, Demographic Monographs, vol. 1 (London: Gordon and Breach).

Thompson, E. P. (1971), 'The Moral Economy of the English Crown in the Eighteenth Century', *P. and P.*, **50**, pp. 77–136.

Thompson, E. P. (1975), *Whigs and Hunters* (London: Allen Lane).

Thompson, E. P. (1975a), 'The Crime of Anonymity', in Hay *et al.* (eds.), 1975, pp. 255–308.

Tobias, J. J. (1967), *Crime and Industrial Society in the Nineteenth Century* (Harmondsworth: Penguin).

Trice, Harrison M. and Roman, Paul Michael (1969–70), 'Delabeling, Relabeling and Alcoholics Anonymous', *Soc. Probs.*, **17**, pp. 538–46.

Truzzi, Marcello (ed.) (1968), *Sociology and Everyday Life* (New Jersey: Prentice-Hall).

Turner, Ralph H. (1971), 'Deviance Avowal as Neutralisation of Commitment', *Soc. Probs.*, **19**, no. 3, pp. 308–21.

Vaihinger, H. (1924), *The Philosophy of 'As If'*, (London: Kegan Paul, Trench, Trubner).

Van Doorn, J. (1975), *Disequilibrium Economics* (London: Macmillan).

Veltfort, H. R. and Lee, G. E. (1943), 'The Coconut Grove Fire: A Study in Scape-goating', *J. of Abnorm. and Soc. Psy.*, **38**, Apr., pp. 138–54.

Vold, George B. (1958), *Theoretical Criminology* (New York: O.U.P.).

Walker, Nigel (1971), *Crimes, Courts and Figures: An Introduction to Criminal Statistics* (Harmondsworth: Penguin).

Walker, Nigel (1977), *Behaviour and Misbehaviour: Explanations and Non-Explanations* (Oxford: B. Blackwell).

Wallerstein, James S. and Wyle, Clement J. (1947), 'Our Law-Abiding Law-Breakers', *Probation*, Apr., pp. 107–13.

Warren, Carol A. B. and Johnson, John M. (1972), 'A Critique of Labeling Theory from the Phenomenological Perspective', in Scott and Douglas (eds.), Ch. 3, pp. 69–92.

Wender, Paul H. (1968), 'Vicious and Virtuous Circles: The Role of Deviation Amplifying Feedback in the Origin and Perpetuation of Behaviour', *Psychiatry*, **31**, no. 4, pp. 309–24.

Wheeler, Stanton (1976), 'Trends and Problems in the Sociological Study of Crime', *Soc. Probs.*, **23**, no. 5, June, pp. 525–34.

Wiles, Paul (1971), 'Criminal Statistics and Sociological Explanations of Crime', in Carson and Wiles (eds.), pp. 174–92.

Wiles, Paul (ed.) (1976), *The Sociology of Crime and Delinquency in Britain*; vol. 2, *The New Criminologies* (London: Martin Robertson).

Wilkins, Leslie T. (1963), 'The Measurement of Crime', *B.J.C.*, **3**, pp. 321–41.

Wilkins, Leslie T. (1964), *Social Deviance* (London: Tavistock).

Wilkins, Leslie T. (1965), 'New Thinking in Criminal Statistics', *J.C.L., C., & P.S.*, **56**, no. 3, pp. 277–84.

Willis, Paul E. (1978), *Profane Culture* (London: R.K.P.).

Winch, Peter (1958), *The Idea of a Social Science and its Relation to Philosophy* (London: R.K.P.).

Wolfgang, Marvin E., Savitz, Leonard and Johnston, Norman (eds.), (1962), *The Sociology of Crime and Delinquency* (London: J. Wiley and Sons).

Wolfgang, Marvin E., Savitz, Leonard and Johnston, Norman (eds.) (1962a), *The Sociology of Punishment and Correction* (London: J. Wiley and Sons).

Wrigley, E. A. (ed.) (1972), *Nineteenth-Century Society: Essays in the Use of Quantitative Methods for the Study of Social Data* (Cambridge: C.U.P.).

Young, Jock (1971), *The Drugtakers* (London: Granada).

Young, Jock (1971a), 'The Role of the Police as Amplifiers of Deviancy, Negotiators of Reality and Translators of Fantasy: Some Consequences of our Present System of Drug Control as seen in Notting Hill', in S. Cohen (ed.), 1971, pp. 27–61.

Young, Malcolm (1977), 'An Examination of Some Aspects of the Developing Perceptions in a Local Community, of non-medical drug use as Marginal, Anti-Structural, Deviant Behaviour' (*Unpub.* B.A. Diss.), (Anthropology Department, Durham University).

Zehr, Howard (1976), *Crime and the Development of Modern Society: Patterns of Criminality in Nineteenth Century Germany and France* (London: Croom Helm).

Index

(Numbers followed by n indicate an endnote reference; those in brackets the location of the full bibliographic citation.)

Akers, Ronald L., 6n, (109)
'Alfred', 51, 73–5, 82, 96n
Anon, 45n, (109)
Armstrong, Gail, and Wilson, Mary, 38n, 98n, (109)
Atkinson, J. Maxwell, 7n, 20, 40n, 42n, (109)

Baker, George W., and Chapman, Dwight W., 94n, (109)
Baldwin, John, and Bottoms, A. E., 17, 107n, (109)
Balk, Alfred, 98n, (109)
Ball, John, with Chester, Lewis, and Perrott, Roy, 96n, 97n, 107n, (109)
Ball, Richard A., 6n, (109)
Bankowski, Zenon, with Mungham, Geoff, and Young, Peter, 7n, (109)
'Barney', 51, 68, 70
'Basil', 51, 52, 62–3, 68–86 passim, 96n
Beattie, J. M., 39n, 43n, (109)
Beattie, R. H., 15, (109)
Becker, Howard S., 4–5, 6n, 7n, 20–1, (109–10)
Bell, Daniel, 16–17, 30, 40n, (110)
'Bert', 51, 62, 82–3
Beyleveld, Deryck, and Wiles, Paul, 7n, (110)
Biderman, Albert D., and Reiss, Albert J., 18, 23, (110)
'Billy', 51, 74–5
Black, Donald J., 16, 18, (110)
'Bob', 51, 69–70, 72, 75, 97n
Bottomley, A. Keith, and Coleman, Clive A., 13, (110)
Box, Stephen, 6n, 18–19, 41n, 107n, (110)
Brennan, William C., 6n, (110)
Broadhead, Robert S., 7n, (110)
Bucher, R., 94n, (110)

Buckner, H. Taylor, 50n, 90, (110)
Bunyan, Tony, 94n, (110)

Campbell, Donald T., and Ross, H. Lawrence, 48n, (110)
Cantril, Hadley, 49n–50n, (110)
Carson, W. G., 41n, (110)
Center, Lawrence J., and Smith, Thomas G., 13, 16, 45n, (110)
Chambliss, William J., 7n, 12, (110–11)
Chapman, Dwight W., 54, (111)
Cicourel, Aaron V., 41n, (111)
'Claude', 51, 62, 82–3
Clay, John, 13, (111)
Cohen, Morris R., 22, (111)
Cohen, Stanley, 6n, 8–10, 12, 37n, 40n, 46n, 55, 84, 107n, 108n, (111)
C.O.I. (Reference Division), 15, (111)
Coleman, Clive A., and Bottomley, A. Keith, 16, 18, 41n, (111)
Conklin, J. E., 45n, (111)
Cooley, Charles Horton, 44n, (111)
Coulter, Jeff, 7n, (111)
'Cyril', 51, 74

Damer, Sean, 38n, (111)
'Dan', 51, 59, 70, 83, 85–6, 94n
Davis, Fred, and Olesen, Virginia, 98n, (111)
Davis, Fred, 6n, (111)
Davis, Nanette J., 7n, (111)
Dickson, Donald T., 47n, (111)
Ditton, Jason, 7n, 47n, 52–3, 67, 70, 77, 79, 93n, 94n, 96n, 99n, 100, 106n, (111–12)
Doleschal, Eugene, and Klapmuts, Nora, 7n, (112)
'Donald', 51, 52–3, 57, 67, 68–76 passim, 86, 98n
'Doug', 51, 57–93 passim, 94n–98n, 106n

Douglas, Jack D., 6n, 16, 45n, (112)
Drabeck, Thomas E., and Quarantelli, Enrico L., 94n, (112)
Du Cane, E. F., 12, 39n, 43n, (112)
Durkheim, Emile, 44n

'Eadley, Mr', 51, 56–83 *passim*, 95n
Emerson, Tony, 17, (112)
Engels, Frederick, 98n, (112)
Ericson, Richard V., 1, 6n, 107n, (112)
Erikson, Kai T., 6n, 24, 43n, 44n, 48n, (112)

'Fatty', 51, 75
Ferracuti, Franco, with Hernandez, Rosita P., and Wolfgang, Marvin E., 16, 41n, (112)
Filstead, William J., 6n, (112)
Fine, Bob, 7n, (112)
Fordham, Peta, 95n, (112)
Friedrichs, Robert W., 6n, (112)
Fritz, Charles E., 94n, (112)

Gattrell, V. A. C., and Hadden, T. B., 13, 29, 39n, 42n, 43n, (113)
'Geoff', 51, 56, 63, 68–81 *passim*, 86, 98n
'George', 51, 77, 79, 82, 95n, 96n
Gibbons, Don C., and Rooney, Elizabeth A., 6n, (113)
Gibbons, Don C., and Jones, Joseph F., 7n, (113)
Gibbs, Jack P., 6n, (113)
Gill, Owen, 49n, (113)
Gillis, John R., 12, 14, (113)
Glasgow University Media Group, 17, (113)
Glass, Gene V., 48n, (113)
Goffman, Erving, 6n, 106n, (113)
Goodde, Erich, 7n, (113)
Gordon, David M., 7n, (113)
Gouldner, Alvin W., 6n, (113)
Gove, Walter R., 6n, (113)

Hagan, John, 6n, 7n, (113)
Hall, Stuart, Critcher, Chas., Jefferson, Tony, Clarke, John, and Roberts, Brian, 13, 40n, 49n, 96n, 98n, 103–5, 108n, (113)
Hanawalt, Barbara, 43n, (113)
Hecker, J. F. C., 49n
Hepworth, Mike, and Turner, Bryan S., 60, (113)
Hindess, Barry, 41n, (113)
Hirschi, Travis, 7n, 107n, (113)
Hirst, Paul Q., 7n, (113)

Hobbs, Albert H., 43n, (113)
Hood, Roger, and Sparks, Richard, 97n, (114)
Horning, Donald M., 107n, (114)
Hughes, Everett C., 53, (114)
Hughes, Patrick H., Barker, Noel W., Crawford, Gail A., and Jaffe, Jerome H., 47n, (114)
Hunt, Leon Gibson, and Chambers, Carl D., 47n–48n

Jacobs, Norman, 49n–50n, (114)
'Jim', 51, 69
Johnson, Donald M., 49n–50n, (114)

Katz, Jack, 6n, (114)
'Keith', 51, 52, 56–83, 85–6, 90–3, 94n–99n, 106n
Kitsuse, John I., 6n, 7n, (114)
Kitsuse, John I., and Cicourel, Aaron V., 17–19, 24, 40n, (114)
Kitsuse, John I., and Dietrick, D. C., 10, (114)
Klapp, Orrin E., 59–60, 99n, (114)
Knutsson, Johannes, 7n, (114)
Kuhn, Thomas S., 1–4, 6n, (114)
Kutchinsky, Berl, 107n, (114)

Laing, R. D., 105, (114)
Laing, R. D., Phillipson, H., and Lee, A. R., 44n, 88, (114)
Larner, Christina, 19, (114)
'Larry', 51, 69, 75
Lemert, Edwin M., 4–6, 6n, 7n, 8, 37n, 45n, 108n, (115)
Levin, Yale, and Lindesmith, Alfred, 6n, (115)
Levitin, Teresa E., 6n, (115)
Liazos, Alexander, 6n, 7n, (115)
Lindesmith, A. R., 37n, (115)
Linebaugh, Peter, 43n, (115)
Lofland, John, 6n, (115)
'Lonny', 51, 77, 82, 94n, 96n

McClintock, F. M., 39n, (115)
McIntosh, Mary, 95n, 96n, (115)
Mackay, Charles, 40n, (115)
Mankoff, Milton, 7n, (115)
Mannheim, Herman, 14, (115)
Manning, Peter K., 7n, 14, (115)
Maruyama, Margoroh, 8, 10, 25–7, 31, 37n, 38n, 45n, 47n, (115)
Masterman, M., 6n, (115)
Mathiesen, Thomas, 107n, (115)

Matza, David, 4–5, 6n, 33–4, 46n–47n, (115)
Mayhew, Henry, 50n, (115)
Mayhew, Henry, and Binny, John, 43n, (115)
Medalia, Nahum Z., and Larsen, Otto N., 49n–50n, 99n, (116)
Megaree, Edwin I., 40n, (116)
Merton, Robert K., 88, 98n, (116)
Mitchell, Wesley Clair, 35, 48n, (116)
'Morrisey, Mr', 51, 56, 70, 75, 78, 82, 96n
Morrison, William Douglas, 39n, 42n, 43n, (116)
Mugford, Stephen K., 7n, (116)

Nettler, Gwynn, 6n, (116)
Newman, Graeme R., 6n, (116)
Noble, J. V., 44n, (116)
N.P.D.S. (Northumbria Police Drug Squad), 30, (116)

Pearce, Frank, 7n, (116)
Pearson, Geoffrey, 6n, 7n, (116)
Phelps, Harold A., 43n, (116)
Philips, David, 43n, (116)
Pine, Vanderlyn R., 94n, (116)
Plummer, Ken, 5, (116)
Potter, Ellen C., 45n–46n, (116)
Priest, Thomas Brian, and McGrath, John H. III, 6n, (116)

Quarantelli, Enrico L., 94n, (116)
Quinney, Richard, 6n, 50n, (116–17)

Radzinowicz, Leon, 14, 43n, (117)
Radzinowicz, Sir Leon, and Wolfgang, Marvin E., 6n, (117)
Rau, Nicholas, 47n, (117)
Rawson, Rawson W., 39n, (117)
Robertson, Roland, and Taylor, Laurie, 9, 37n, (117)
Rock, Paul, 6n, 7n, (117)
Rock, Paul, and McIntosh, Mary, 6n, (117)
Rodgers, Joseph W., and Buffalo, M. D., 6n, (117)
Roshier, Bob, 39n, 43n, (117)
Ross, H. Lawrence, with Campbell, Donald T., and Glass, Gene V., 96n, 107n, (117)
Rotenberg, Mordechai, 6n, (117)
Rubington, Earl, and Weinberg, Martin S., 6n, (117)

Samaha, Joel, 43n, (117)

Scheff, Thomas J., 6n, 7n, 8, 38n, 45n, (118)
Schervish, Paul G., 7n, (118)
Schuler, Edgar A., and Parenton, Vernon J., 48n, (118)
Schur, Edwin M., 6n, 7n, 37n, 42n, 108n, (118)
Scull, Andrew T., 15, 96n, 103–4, 106n, (118)
Seidman, David, and Couzens, Michael, 16–17, 50n, (118)
Sellin, Thorsten, 19, 21, 41n, (118)
Short, James F., 43n, (118)
Silver, Allan, 45n, (118)
Skolnick, Jerome, 33, (118)
'Smarteagh, Mr', 51, 59–72 *passim*, 78–9, 85, 94n
Sparks, Richard F., Genn, Hazel G., and Dodd, David J., 13–15, (118)
Spitzer, Steven, 7n, (118)
Steadman-Jones, Gareth, 7n, (118)
Sudnow, David, 6n, (118)
Sumner, Colin, 7n, (118)
Sykes, Gresham M., 7n, (118)

Talese, Gay, 96n, (119)
Taylor, Ian, and Taylor, Laurie, 6n, (119)
Taylor, Ian, Walton, Paul, and Young, Jock, 7n, 103, (119)
Taylor, Laurie, 6n, 10, 37n
Thio, Alex, 7n, (119)
Thomas, Dorothy Swaine, 43n, 47n
Thompson, E. P., 12, 40n, 43n, (119)
Tobias, J. J., 14, (119)
Trice, Harrison M., and Roman, Paul Michael, 6n, (119)
Turner, Ralph H., 6n, (119)

Vaihinger, H., 22, 41n, (119)
Van Doorn, J., 44n, (119)
Veltfort, H. R., and Lee, G. E., 94n, (119)
Vold, George B., 42n, (119)

Walker, Nigel, 7n, 16, 21, (119)
Wallerstein, James S., and Wyle, Clement J., 13, (119)
'Wally', 51, 59–60, 68–78 *passim*, 98n
Warren, Carol A. B., and Johnson, John M., 7n, (119)
Wender, Paul H., 44n, (119)
Wheeler, Stanton, 7n, (119)
Wiles, Paul, 7n, 39n, (119)
Wilkins, Leslie T., 8–12, 19, 24–7, 31, 37n–38n, 41n–42n, 43n, 45n, 97n, (120)

Willis, Paul E., 98n, (120)
Winch, Peter, 21, (120)
Wolfgang, Marvin E., with Savitz, Leonard, and Johnston, Norman, 6n, (120)

Young, Jock, 7n, 9, 30, 33, 37n, 38n, 88–9, 98n, 103, (120)
Young, Malcolm, 14, (120)

Zehr, Howard, 43n, (120)